D1154263

UNDERSTANDING
DIANE JOHNSON

UNDERSTANDING

DIANE JOHNSON

Carolyn A. Durham

The University of South Carolina Press

© 2012 University of South Carolina

Published by the University of South Carolina Press
Columbia, South Carolina 29208

www.sc.edu/uscpress

Manufactured in the United States of America

21 20 19 18 17 16 15 14 13 12   10 9 8 7 6 5 4 3 2 1

Library of Congress Cataloging-in-Publication Data

Durham, Carolyn A.
    Understanding Diane Johnson / Carolyn A. Durham.
        p. cm. — (Understanding contemporary American literature)
    Includes bibliographical references and index.
    ISBN 978-1-61117-075-7 (cloth : alk. paper)
    1. Johnson, Diane, 1934– —Criticism and interpretation. I. Title.
    PS3560.O3746Z58 2012
    813'.54—dc23

                                                    2012008084

This book was printed on a reycled paper with 30 percent postconsumer
waste content.

For John, Deb, and Diane herself

CONTENTS

SERIES EDITOR'S PREFACE

The Understanding Contemporary American Literature series was founded by the estimable Matthew J. Bruccoli (1931–2008), who envisioned these volumes as guides or companions for students as well as good nonacademic readers, a legacy that will continue as new volumes are developed to fill in gaps among the nearly one hundred series volumes published to date and to embrace a host of new writers only now making their marks on our literature.

As Professor Bruccoli explained in his preface to the volumes he edited, because much influential contemporary literature makes special demands, "the word *understanding* in the titles was chosen deliberately. Many willing readers lack an adequate understanding of how contemporary literature works; that is, of what the author is attempting to express and the means by which it is conveyed." Aimed at fostering this understanding of good literature and good writers, the criticism and analysis in the series provide instruction in how to read certain contemporary writers—explicating their material, language, structures, themes, and perspectives—and facilitate a more profitable experience of the works under discussion.

In the twenty-first century, Professor Bruccoli's prescience gives us an avenue to publish expert critiques of significant contemporary American writing. The series continues to map the literary landscape and provide both instruction and enjoyment. Future volumes will seek to introduce new voices alongside canonized favorites, to chronicle the changing literature of our times, and to remain, as Professor Bruccoli conceived, contemporary in the best sense of the word.

Linda Wagner-Martin, Series Editor

ACKNOWLEDGMENTS

I am grateful to the College of Wooster for supporting the research leave in 2010–11 that allowed me to complete this book and for providing funding from the Henry Luce III Fund for Distinguished Scholarship, which permitted me to interview Diane Johnson in Paris on a number of occasions. I thank Diane Johnson for her willingness to speak with me on a wide variety of topics over a period of several years and especially while I was completing this project. One of the great pleasures in writing this book has been the opportunity to get to know the writer as well as her work. The Filmstrip Acquisitions Endowment from the Harry Ransom Center also provided support for my research. I thank all the librarians and staff members at the Ransom Center, and specifically Richard Workman and Pat Fox, for their courtesy and assistance during my research fellowship. I am grateful to my students at the College of Wooster for the many ways in which they have challenged and encouraged my thinking and my scholarship. In particular Frances (Boo) Flynn patiently helped me track down references and reviews and Katharine Tatum's senior thesis reflected our shared interest in the works of Diane Johnson.

I thank Diane Johnson for permission to quote from our conversations, and I thank the Harry Ransom Center at the University of Texas at Austin for making various materials available.

CHAPTER 1

Understanding Diane Johnson

In the course of her forty-five-year writing career, Diane Johnson has been variously described, including in her own words, as a comic novelist, a novelist of manners, an American novelist, an international novelist, and a travel novelist. Although she does not write poetry or drama, the diversity of her nonfiction work, which includes literary criticism, biography, book reviews, travelogues, and essays, rivals that of her fiction in range and complexity. Although she is best known as a novelist, Johnson's work constitutes an authentic oeuvre in which her key interests, notably the concepts of "America" and of "Americanness," recur in different forms and contexts to enrich the reader's understanding. Because she is a comic novelist who addresses serious social problems, a quintessentially American novelist who characteristically populates her fiction with foreigners and expatriates, and a novelist of manners who reinvents a fictional form commonly viewed as both outmoded and fundamentally alien to the American novel, her career embodies many paradoxes and ironies.

In an initial contradiction, Johnson's lifelong engagement with questions of cultural difference directly contrasts with her own heritage and upbringing. Born in 1934 in Moline, Illinois, the author, like her parents and grandparents before her, grew up in the Midwest in a "family with absolutely no ethnic consciousness." In comparison to the colorful relatives, holiday customs, and unusual food enjoyed by classmates of primarily Scandinavian descent, Johnson, a "DAR WASP" with ancestors who arrived on the *Mayflower* and fought in the American Revolution, recalls the disappointment she felt at her own "boring background." This early experience as a cultural outsider and Johnson's resultant sense of herself as a "default American" suggest that the novelist's interest in exploring national identity from within a cross-cultural framework and through the eyes of a stranger was developed at a very early age.[1]

If Johnson's middle-class upbringing in a bedroom community for "the executive class" of John Deere is consistent with the largely privileged background common to writers interested in customs and manners, it did not necessarily augur a future as a novelist. Johnson's assertion that she has "always been a writer" is confirmed both by the childhood diaries she kept with unusual fidelity and the "first novel" she remembers completing at the age of nine, but at this point in her life it never occurred to her that writing might be a career, let alone her own career. She did not know any living authors, nor, in fact, had she read any, even though her early experience as "a Midwestern child from a rather bookish and cultivated home" turned her into a passionate reader.[2] She read Jane Austen and was particularly fond of Victorian literature, notably the fiction of William Makepeace Thackeray and Anthony Trollope; Henry James figured especially prominently among the few American novelists she encountered while working her way through the local Carnegie Library's list of the "World's Great Novels." This early immersion in the books of writers renowned for their comedic and satirical treatment of society and whose works serve to define the novel of manners clearly influenced Johnson's own fictional practice. Similarly her love of reading remains evident in her extensive nonfiction writing, some of which is devoted to the beloved authors of her youth whom she continues to reread on a regular basis. Even an early interest in foreign travel and in France in particular is evident in the books that she read in childhood. The Francophile librarian in Moline also introduced Johnson to the historical adventures of Alexandre Dumas *père,* whose d'Artagnan emerges from the pages of *The Three Musketeers* to lead the reader through Paris in *Into a Paris Quarter* (2005). In *Natural Opium: Some Travelers' Tales* (1993), Johnson traces her adult interest in travel writing back to other favorite childhood stories, Phyllis Ayer Sowers's *Let's Go 'round the World with Bob and Betty* (1934) and *Two Years before the Mast* (1869), Richard Henry Dana's classic tale of a sea voyage.

Although Johnson did finally encounter contemporary American fiction when she began her studies at Stephens College in Columbia, Missouri, in 1951, she essentially wrote only to maintain her diary and to complete class assignments. Johnson had taken art classes throughout childhood, and she expected to major in studio art, following in the footsteps of her mother, Frances Elder Lain, who was an art teacher. In fact although Johnson's ongoing interest in painting informs the setting, characterization, and metaphoric structure of several of her novels, it was her father's profession that ultimately played the more determinate role in her life and career. Dolph Lain abandoned his position as a high school principal to pursue a passion for motion pictures, an interest that Johnson's adolescent diaries suggest that she already shared and which subsequently led her into screenwriting. As a result of his work as an audiovisual consultant to college and university libraries, Johnson's father met B. Lamar Johnson, a Stephens College dean, who helped determine Johnson's choice of college; more important, he became her father-in-law two years later when at the age of nineteen she married his son and namesake, B. Lamar Johnson Jr., in July 1953. Johnson's husband-to-be was studying medicine at the University of Missouri, and she was introduced to a community whose practices and ethics figure importantly in her writing of fiction.

An experience that in retrospect might reasonably be described as epiphanic, given the actors and the context, occurred early in the summer of Johnson's marriage. A short story she had written at Stephens won a contest that earned her one of twenty guest editorships for the annual college edition of *Mademoiselle* magazine. On her first trip east of the Mississippi, the "country-mouse teen-ager terrified by New York" lived and worked alongside Sylvia Plath, who later immortalized her version of June 1953 in *The Bell Jar*.[3] Although Johnson remembers having little in common with her sophisticated, career-oriented fellow editors, epitomized by the gifted and ambitious Plath, her example led Johnson to the realization that writing was not an easy and frivolous pastime but rather real work, requiring serious commitment and careful revision: "I realized that if you took pains with your writing, you could make art, and that the rather facile little stories I had dashed off for my English classes or the school magazine were probably not art. It was, in fact, the example of 'Sunday at the Mintons,' Sylvia Plath's winning story in the Guest Editor contest, that made that point to me and changed my life"— "though not," Johnson adds, "immediately"; at the time this insight led no further than a brief attraction to journalism.[4] It took a second encounter with another book enthusiast, a university librarian at UCLA, where Johnson worked to support her new husband while he completed medical school, to concretize her desire and determination to write.

What happened next might today seem like an ironic accident of fate borrowed from one of Johnson's own domestic comedies, but early marriage and motherhood were entirely normal in the late 1950s. In the next six years— spent first at the University of Utah, where her husband interned and she completed her B.A., and then back in Los Angeles, where he took up residency— Johnson had four children, two in the same year. In 1956 a son was born in January and a daughter in December; a second daughter followed in July

1960, and a second son in February 1962. Johnson's experience during their early childhood no doubt provided firsthand knowledge of the traditional female life that she satirized in her early novels. Johnson also discovered, however, that writing was an ideal "cottage industry" for someone caring for young children, and she completed her first and only unpublished novel during this period.[5] "Runes" is also the only one of her works that can be described as both young adult fiction and an academic novel. It is also the only story whose primary setting is in the Midwest. Johnson's female heroine is an ethnologist specializing in folklore, whose unraveling of a mystery, translation of an ancient Nordic manuscript, and discovery of an original Viking community in Michigan demonstrates that from the beginning of her career Johnson was interested in cultural difference, travel, the formation of America's national identity, and the detective novel.

Johnson's first three published novels are all set in Southern California, which led to an initial attempt on the part of reviewers to label her as a regional or a California novelist, quickly followed, no doubt as an almost inevitable result of her sex and the ideological context of the times, by a desire to identify her as a woman's or a feminist writer. More accurately *Fair Game*, published in 1965, inaugurated Johnson's practice of setting her fiction wherever she happened to be living; and the satiric adventure of a young woman's struggles to balance not only love and ambition but also the four men who desire her establishes Johnson's interest in gender politics and in relationships between men and women. Three years later, in *Loving Hands at Home* (1968), Johnson's heroine rebels against the staid Mormon family into which she has married, allowing the novelist to explore cross-cultural conflict within American society. Johnson's interest in Mormonism was sparked by her friendship at the University of Utah with a Mormon classmate whom she had met during their guest editorship at *Mademoiselle*. With a third novel published in 1971, Johnson was engaged on what already promised to be a highly productive career. Inspired by the Bel Air–Brentwood fire of November 1961, *Burning* focuses on a highly conventional but increasingly disillusioned and estranged middle-class couple who encounter, in the course of a single day, every possible stereotypical character and situation of Southern California culture. Johnson's first three novels also established a career-long pattern of alternating between first-person and third-person narration, of bringing back characters from earlier novels, and of approaching realistic problems and situations with irony and wit.

Although none of Johnson's novels is strongly autobiographical, she has called *Loving Hands at Home,* whose Mormon family is based in part on her own in-laws, her "discontented wife novel," and her first three works of fiction all satirize traditional marriage. Johnson and her first husband ended their fifteen-year marriage in 1968, and Johnson remarried in May of the same year. Her second husband, John Frederic Murray, was also a doctor and a professor of medicine at UC San Francisco, leaving intact the novelist's ties to a world of medical professionals. Johnson herself now had a doctorate, having found time during her period of marital discontent to complete an M.A. (1966) and a Ph.D. (1968) at UCLA. Her specialization in Victorian literature confirmed the reading passions of her childhood, and it is primarily as a reader that Johnson has made the greatest use of her professional competence as a literary historian and critic. Just as Johnson's decision to pursue graduate studies was motivated less by her love of literature than by the need for a young housewife and mother to seek an independent means of support, so too she has found the writing of book reviews, essays, and scholarly introductions to be a more satisfying use of her expertise than traditional teaching and research. Although Johnson was a tenured full professor at UC Davis and taught nineteenth-century British literature, the Gothic novel, and eventually creative writing for almost twenty years (1968–87), she has always defined herself as a writer, not a professor, and she took repeated leaves of absence and sabbaticals during her term of appointment in order to focus on the writing of fiction.

Johnson's single foray into academic scholarship is therefore particularly intriguing. In the first place, she chose to write her doctoral dissertation on the poetry of George Meredith, focusing on a literary genre with which she had no personal experience. In the second place, rather than pursuing her work on Meredith in keeping with what is standard practice for a recent Ph.D., she used her dissertation as a springboard to the writing of *The True History of the First Mrs. Meredith and Other Lesser Lives*. In addition, although the novelist herself had never shown any interest in writing experimental fiction, the literary biography of Mary Ellen Meredith is most remarkable for its innovative form, which is of far greater interest than its actual subject matter. *Lesser Lives* earned Johnson a National Book Award nomination for biography in 1973.

The questions that Johnson raises in *Lesser Lives* about biography as a genre and the prominence its practice subjectively confers on certain people to the exclusion of others also play an important role in her next novel. Published in 1974, *The Shadow Knows*, the first of her fictional works to be published by Knopf and the first of three novels set in northern California, can be deemed her breakthrough book. Johnson considers the first-person story of the divorced mother of four young children struggling to complete a graduate degree to be the most autobiographical of her fictional works. Notably two of the caretakers of the narrator's children whose "lesser lives" become central in the novel are closely based on women who performed the same work for Johnson. Indeed a passage in her personal diary from 1964 bears a striking resemblance to the fictional version it later informed. Filled with ironic allusions to the literary conventions of the murder mystery, including conversations with an imaginary "Famous Inspector," *The Shadow Knows* also reflects its author's ongoing engagement with the detective genre.

In 1978 Johnson's *Lying Low* brought her a second nomination for the National Book Award, and the sophistication of voice and narrative technique characteristic of her fifth novel suggests that the writing of *Lesser Lives* influenced her thinking about fiction. In contrast to *The Shadow Knows*, *Lying Low* is no doubt the least personally motivated of Johnson's novels and the one in which the humor is the darkest. Although she continues to focus on female characters who live largely invisible, marginal lives, Johnson now uses their particular circumstances to comment on American society more generally and especially on America as a culture prone to violence and terrorism. America was also in many ways the central concern of *Terrorists and Novelists,* a book of collected essays nominated for a Pulitzer Prize in 1983. Although most of the essays included in this compilation were commissioned, read as a whole the work offers the reader both a figurative biography of Johnson and an implied aesthetics as well as further confirmation of the diversity of her concerns and the morality of her authorial voice. It also provides clear evidence of the broad curiosity and the desire to explore different forms of writing that continued to influence Johnson's career.

When Stanley Kubrick first contacted the novelist about the possibility of a film collaboration, his interest appeared to be in an adaptation of *The Shadow Knows*. Instead Johnson and Kubrick cowrote the script for *The Shining,* a horror movie based on a Stephen King novel, which was released in 1980 to become an instant classic. Johnson's contribution was primarily literary rather than cinematic, drawing upon her knowledge of Gothic literature and her talent for writing convincing dialogue. Her friendship with Kubrick also provided the inspiration for the character of a fictional filmmaker in one of her later novels, and although their original plans fell through, Johnson herself eventually wrote multiple drafts of a screenplay for *The Shadow Knows*. She also collaborated with the director Mike Nichols on the scenario for a planned remake of *Grand Hotel* and wrote several additional screenplays for United Artists in the 1980s. One of these, *Two Lives,* based on works by Lillian Hellman, was inspired by the research she did for her second biography, *Dashiell Hammett: A Life,* published in 1983. Although *Dashiell Hammett* is ostensibly much more traditional in form than *Lesser Lives* and demonstrates Johnson's ability to write a conventional biography, her account of the life of a writer jailed for "un-American activities" can also, ironically, once again be read as a history of America.

Although none of Johnson's screenplays other than *The Shining* was ever produced, the novelist found her work in film to be beneficial to her writing of fiction. An increased interest in plotting, as opposed to characterization, can be dated to this experience, and Johnson also found that working with Kubrick altered her methods of composition. She began to conceive of the episodes of her novels as distinct narrative units on the model of the sequential images of the cinematic storyboard. Some of the effects of these changes can be seen in *Health and Happiness,* published in 1990 and the last of her works to be set exclusively in California—indeed in the United States. Johnson's clever satire of the life of a large metropolitan hospital and the multiple mistakes and misdeeds of its staff was the logical consequence of her long association, as a result of her two marriages, with the medical world.

John Murray's profession is also responsible for the next stage of Johnson's career. In 1993 she published *Natural Opium: Some Travelers' Tales,* a collection of observations and anecdotes gleaned during a series of trips on which she accompanied her husband, a specialist in infectious diseases. In 1988 the receipt of a five-year grant from the American Academy of Arts and Letters for the Harold and Mildred Strauss Living Award had allowed her to retire from teaching, leaving her the freedom to fulfill her childhood dreams of travel. Although none of the tales in *Natural Opium* is set in France, Murray's work with international health organizations based in Paris subsequently led to a change in Johnson's living arrangements that also determined the setting of her next three novels. Since 1994 the couple has spent at least six months each year in their apartment near Saint-Germain-des-Prés, the neighborhood that Johnson invites her readers to explore in *Into a Paris Quarter.* Her continued engagement with questions of national identity, now viewed from within an explicitly cross-cultural framework, led reviewers to credit her with the resurrection and reinvention of the international novel inherited from Edith Wharton and Henry James, who still figures among Johnson's favorite novelists.

Le Divorce, the first volume in what eventually became a Franco-American trilogy of novels, not only earned Johnson her third National Book Award nomination but greatly increased her reading audience, even before James Ivory's film adaptation was released in 2003. By her own admission, the novelist found herself for the first time in her life seated next to people on airplanes and at dinner parties who had read her book. With the publication of *Le Mariage* and *L'Affaire* in 2000 and 2003 respectively, Johnson solidified her reputation as the modern interpreter of the classic plot of the American abroad. The timelessness of her subtle and witty treatment of the adventures of three young women who fall in and out of love both in and with France and the French combined with a somewhat serendipitous timeliness as a result of the increasing tensions that developed between the United States and France in the first decade of the twenty-first century. As a result Johnson's fiction became more overtly political during this period, and the legal profession replaced medicine as a primary target of her satire.

While contemporary political concerns no doubt increased popular interest in Johnson's Franco-American trilogy, the completion of an earlier novel was almost derailed by current events. *Persian Nights* was initially inspired by a three-month medical exchange that took Johnson and Murray to Iran in 1978 in the days leading up to the collapse of Shah Pahlavi's regime. Johnson put the unfinished novel aside during the 1979–80 Iranian hostage crisis and returned to it only when her second trip to Egypt in the early 1980s revived her interest in Islam and the Middle East. The novel earned Johnson her second Pulitzer Prize nomination in 1987, and its concern with Muslim fundamentalism and the condition of women in Islamic society has become increasingly relevant in recent years. Such issues have also become increasingly controversial in the wake of 9/11 and the wars in Iraq and Afghanistan. Her most recent novel to date, *Lulu in Marrakech*, published in 2008, is a satirical treatment of the dangers of American ignorance of the Islamic world and the ineptness that results from national naïveté and pretension. The two novels that Johnson has set outside of the United States and Europe marked the expansion of her interest in detective fiction to include the political thriller and the spy novel.

As of the spring of 2011, Johnson's most recent writing announces a metaphorical return not only to America but also to the region in which she was born and raised. She is completing a memoir, a "meditation on the Midwest," which will include a variety of pieces, unified by the continuity of the narrative voice, on subjects ranging from house parties and bridge games to her family's military history. The immediate impetus to complete the autobiography comes from the concurrence between Johnson's current age and that of her great-great-grandmother, who in 1876, at the age of seventy-six, began to keep a diary that serves as one source for the memoir. Johnson is also planning a new novel that in structure and tone will be modeled to some extent on Anthony Trollope's *The Way We Live Now* (1875), a satire of greed and corruption inspired by the novelist's return to England from Australia. Johnson described the project, which will feature an older heroine who comes back to the United States after living for some time in Europe, as "eerily parallel" to Trollope's novel.[6]

In the course of a single interview, Johnson describes herself as "a comic novelist," "a novelist of manners," "an American novelist," "an international novelist," and "a natural travel writer." The only potential designation she rejects in the course of the conversation is that of "expatriate novelist," affirming that she "writes as an American for an American audience."[7] It seems fittingly ironic, then, fully in keeping with the particular nature of the humor that informs Johnson's work, that critics and reviewers have sought from the beginning of her career to relegate her to different and far more restrictive categories than those she finds accurate. Paradoxically, given her peripatetic life, the most persistent of these has been that of "regional novelist." The first critical reference to Johnson as a typically Californian writer dates from 1983, when she figured among "ten of the best" in an anthology titled *Women Writers of the West Coast,* and one of the relatively rare critical essays devoted to her work appeared in *San Francisco in Fiction: Essays in a Regional Literature* as late as 1995, almost ten years after *Persian Nights,* set in Iran, was nominated for a Pulitzer Prize. As Johnson, who only moved to Los Angeles in early adulthood, put it at the time, "It's puzzling to find yourself being categorized as a regional writer of some sort from a region not your own."[8] In addition the novelist, who was born and raised in Illinois, argues that midwesterners, once uprooted, are permanently displaced: "I think I've always been a bit deracinated as a Midwesterner. Like other Midwesterners, once I left the Midwest and its very nourishing and womb-like atmosphere, I felt a bit like a stranger." Moreover it is paradoxically in California, where Johnson lived for most of the next forty years and where she still spends some months each year, that she has always felt least at home: "I don't fit in with a completely Californian lifestyle or way of feeling things."[9]

Yet, in keeping with the pattern of her own life, Johnson does in fact populate her novels with Californians, initially with characters who have moved to California from elsewhere and later with those who have permanently or temporarily left their native California behind. It is precisely this potential for relocation and redefinition, which Johnson associates with California, that makes her work consistent with what David Fine and Paul Skenazy describe as "an unusual form of American regionalism" in their introduction to *San Francisco in Fiction: Essays in a Regional Literature.*[10] The two editors of the collection describe a literary version of California created by "writers who come from elsewhere," which exists as a space of "cultural confrontations, assimilations, and resistances" and whose development via a process of "grafting or hybridization" produces less a place than "an adventure, a kind of border crossing" for a "hybrid or hyphenated population."[11] It is just such an image of a mythic and metaphoric California, now equated with America itself, that Johnson has explored throughout her career, first by its direct inscription in those novels set in Los Angeles or San Francisco and then by its displacement to Europe and the Middle East in her more recent international works. In all instances Johnson's California remains what Wallace Stegner has identified as "America only more so" and what the novelist herself has called "if not anywhere in America, [then] the future of America."[12]

Thus, although Johnson has consistently—and understandably, given the narrowness of focus regionalism often implies—sought to escape what she has called "the stigma of 'place' novels," the *concept* of place is always key to the construction of her literary world.[13] By writing about America in the context of other societies, many of them internal, and from the perspective of outsiders, many of them fellow citizens, Johnson confirms a theory outlined by the literary critic and cultural historian Alfred Kazin, whose own writings often focused on the immigrant experience in America. Kazin explains "the essential sense of place" that he attributes to the American literary tradition by the fact that "we are strangers to each other and that each writer describes his own world to strangers living in the same land."[14] In her most recent fiction, Johnson's effort to contribute to cross-cultural and international understanding by helping Americans see themselves and their country as they are seen by others adapts this tradition to the contemporary context of an increasingly globalized and mobile world. Her description of *Natural Opium: Some Travelers' Tales* as a collection of essays about "the existential condition of *being a traveler*" ultimately describes all of her books, in which, as she goes on to note, "travel brings us as nothing else does to a sense of ourselves."[15]

Although Johnson consistently focuses on the importance of place as a source of meaning in fiction, she finds description to be the most onerous task she faces as a novelist. The configuration of her texts, however, is often of particular interest to Johnson, and she frequently uses spatial metaphors to describe her process of writing and revision: "I think of my books as having shape, as having parts which I move around. I even envision the process in a spatial way, in three dimensions somehow."[16] In keeping with her preoccupation with geographical dislocation, existential travel, and constant mobility, Johnson has also struggled to articulate a theory of narrative based on a notion of the space in between: "The relevant or salient thing happens and it's not Event A or Event B but it's in the space between A and B. . . . It's in some kind of dynamic that is generated. . . . It's sudden affect of cause and effect, which is where I think the excitement of a narrative or the interest of a narrative happens. . . . It's not that someone climbs up the ladder and then someone pulls out the ladder; it's in that perception you have that the ladder's going to fall where a kind of emotion is generated—suspense, apprehension, understanding, whatever—that is an important part of narrative." It is characteristic of the impressive breadth of knowledge often evident in Johnson's work that she has drawn on a number of different analogies in an attempt to clarify her thinking. She has, for example, variously compared this phenomenon to an electrical spark, to the synapse between two nerve cells, and to the process of editing film.[17]

Although Johnson is obviously a woman who writes about women, her reputation as a women's writer or a feminist novelist, the second most frequent category to which she has been relegated by reviewers and critics, may actually stem more from the fact that her early career coincided with a period of rapid societal change and with the rise of second-wave feminism than from either her own sex or that of her fictional characters. That Johnson is a feminist is for her a truism: "I regard myself as a feminist, as any nice woman would be. I don't see how another attitude is possible to any serious person." She does not, however, regard herself as a feminist writer: "To be any kind of a writer with an 'ism' would make it harder to be an artist, and art is hard enough. Of course my books have women in them, and women's problems because those are the ones I know about. I resent, as many women writers surely have, the current view that seems to hold that men write 'literature,' but women write 'feminist' literature, just because the former have, likely, male, the latter female protagonists; and if a book by a man has a female protagonist it is still excused." In her desire to be seen simply as a writer, Johnson recalls such nineteenth-century predecessors as Jane Austen and the Brontës and such older French counterparts as Nathalie Sarraute and Marguerite Duras more than she does the female compatriots of her own generation. Although she resembles the latter in her acknowledgment that women may treat different subjects and use different metaphors, including the house or the quilt, both of which appeared in many openly feminist works of the seventies and eighties, she does not understand "why people of both sexes can't have access to these common backgrounds and myths without saying that some are for both sexes but some are for women only and, perforce, less worthy."[18]

Although all four of Johnson's first-person novels (*Loving Hands at Home, The Shadow Knows, Le Divorce,* and *Lulu in Marrakech*) are narrated by women, the majority of her eleven novels are recounted in the third person, and the framing consciousness is as likely to be male as female. Notably we see the heroine of her first novel, *Fair Game,* only through the

eyes of four male protagonists; *Burning* is alternately told from the perspectives of a husband and a wife; and *Health and Happiness* accords a leading
role to its principal male character. Gender roles and relationships and the
complex dynamics of domestic and family life are central concerns of Johnson's work, but her interest in how people behave is broadly conceived, and
as a satirical novelist, she envisions all human beings, regardless of sex or gender, as in some ways flawed. Her characteristic juxtaposition of different
points of view allows the reader to hear the often ironic voice of the author
as well. In general Johnson tends to adopt the point of view of characters who
are literally or metaphorically travelers, strangers or outsiders whose lack of
knowledge, understanding, or appreciation for different customs and values
allows them to see what longtime members of a given group or residents of a
particular place no longer perceive. In this way her narrative strategies recall
those of such eighteenth-century satirical writers as Voltaire (*L'Ingénu, Candide*) or Montesquieu (*Persian Letters*), whose interests also lay in cultural
concerns, including the critique of traditional assumptions about gender.

Some of the multiple designations that Johnson not only is willing to
accept but also uses to describe her own work nonetheless prove interestingly
paradoxical. The most significant of these has to do with the interplay of tone,
genre, and national identity; as Johnson has said: "I think of myself as a comic
novelist, I guess—or a novelist of manners" and "I, of course, see myself as
an American novelist, one who has a slightly different focus."[19] Much of the
critical and theoretical work devoted to "comedy of manners" assumes that
the term, like *comedy* itself, can be accurately applied only to dramatic works,
notably to those of English playwrights ranging from Shakespeare to Oscar
Wilde to Noël Coward. Although Johnson has never written for the theater,
this association is all the same surprisingly useful for an understanding of her
fiction. Dialogue figures particularly prominently in her novels and is frequently key to the creation of humorous situations. Similarly her novels
include secondary characters whose exaggerated traits and predominantly
comic function recall the stock figures conventional in comedy. In addition,
Johnson practices a temporal and spatial concentration that recalls that of
Molière, Pierre Beaumarchais, and Pierre de Marivaux, the French masters of
the comedy of manners. As in their plays, her novels also tend to culminate in
a communal scene that brings most or all of a large cast of characters back on
stage for a final confrontation.

The problematic of the novel of manners, however, extends well beyond
its initial identification with drama. Despite the prominence that the works
of James and Wharton necessarily play in any critical discussion of the form,
the debate over its essential foreignness to American letters clearly remained

unresolved well into the second half of the twentieth century. In 1972, for example, James W. Tuttleton prefaced *The Novel of Manners in America* by confronting in a series of epigraphs the multiple literary critics and theorists who challenged the very possibility of its existence as a significant form of American fiction. Lionel Trilling, for example, claims that the novel of manners "has never really established itself in America," and Richard Chase argues that "there are no manners in America to observe." John Brooks is the only critic cited who takes the opposing point of view and in so doing articulates the task facing Johnson: "The job of the novelist of manners has simply become more complex, more challenging, and more important. . . . Not the least of the jobs of the contemporary novelist is that of rescuing American society from the charge that it doesn't exist."[20] In a direct response to Alexis de Tocqueville, whose celebrated travels through America lie at the origin of the negative views expressed above, Johnson notes in a 1982 essay that the best books about America are now being written by Americans rather than Europeans as a result of a new awareness of diversity and a new sense of complexity, arising "not so much from character as from having a complicated place to be in."[21]

Like other practitioners of the novel of manners, whose central concern is the way people behave in a social context, Johnson is especially interested in relations between the sexes. It follows that marriage, adultery, and divorce figure prominently among the subjects whose complications interest her the most and that also allow for consideration of the social dynamics of appearance and reality. In this context it is clear that the ironic humor and satirical tone characteristic of the novel of manners do not preclude the treatment of serious topics. Indeed what may best distinguish novels of manners, including Johnson's, from their theatrical counterparts stems significantly from the former's ambiguously happy endings and the incorporation of potentially tragic events. Johnson explicitly notes that her self-definition as a novelist of manners "implies comedy of errors and tragedy."[22] Gordon Milne confirms this contradiction of tone and focus in *The Sense of Society: A History of the American Novel of Manners:* "the novel of manners is at best a seriocomic exploration of the conflicts between ethical standards and social virtues."[23] Several of Johnson's novels end with the death of important characters (*Lying Low, Le Divorce, Lulu in Marrakech*); others treat various forms of violence and destruction, including natural disaster (*Burning, L'Affaire*), rape (*The Shadow Knows*), political revolution (*Persian Nights*), and serious illness (*Health and Happiness*). An appreciation of the particular nature of Johnson's humor is therefore key to the understanding of her work.

Critical opposition to an American novel of manners, as Tuttleton points out, has much to do with what are assumed to be the consequences of life in an egalitarian society: "[One] objection is based on the claim that America lacks the social differences which are the sine qua non of the novel of manners. Can the novel of manners flourish in a democratic country which supposedly lacks adequate social density and a clearly stratified and stable class structure?"[24] Milne concludes that changing social mores further complicate the situation: "The genre presents some special problems in the present 'fluid' era, to be sure. The characters of the current 'open society' seem less susceptible to precise definition. . . . Modern society is too mobile for positive identification with a locale."[25] The novels that Johnson sets in California offer an intriguing solution to the dilemma posed by class and geographical instability. As places, as much as characters or plots, figure increasingly as the protagonists of her fiction, the novelist takes the reader on a satirical tour of a series of generic spaces—the corporate world in *Fair Game,* the public housing complex in *The Shadow Knows,* the boardinghouse in *Lying Low,* the modern health care institution in *Health and Happiness*—that enable her to address the broadly social, moral, and cultural issues that inform her tragicomic novels of manners. Johnson focuses on societal structures whose functioning is dependent on rules, rank, and codes in order to create a context within democratic America in which to explore the dynamics of those who are "out of place."

Significantly, however, *Health and Happiness,* whose events unfold in the carefully contained and socially stratified world of a hospital, was the last of Johnson's novels to be set in the United States. By the time of its composition, she too had begun to confront the difficulty of addressing the questions that interested her within the context of American society: "In a big, open society like ours, you can no longer write novels of manners . . . in which the jokes or turns of plot depend on who is out of place. There is no place."[26] In *Persian Nights, Lulu in Marrakech,* and especially in her Franco-American trilogy, Johnson repositions her American novels of manners within the tradition of the international novel. The explicitly cross-cultural context of her recent fiction allows her to explore cultural differences and to foreground the ambiguities of place and identity, what she has called "the curious inability of Americans abroad to stop being American."[27] In keeping with the inspiration she always gains from her own geographical location, her recent work also confirms an interest in the relationship between Europe and the United States, often explored metaphorically through the complicated liaisons of lovers of different nationalities. In *L'Affaire,* for example, which has at its center an affair between an idealistic American woman and an anti-American Frenchman, Johnson sought "to get at that indefinable prejudice that Europeans have against Americans and Americans' rather strange longing for Europe and what they term 'culture,' which is something that James went into endlessly."[28]

Johnson's recent work is particularly indebted to James and Wharton, two other displaced American writers whose work she regularly rereads. Unlike either Wharton, however, whose characters suffer as a result of cultural deracination, or James, whose characters share his personal frustration at the difficulty of penetrating European society, Johnson sees the impossibility of cultural assimilation as beneficial for a novelist: "I've decided that it's probably impossible to integrate into a foreign culture. This is probably less painful for a writer who, by temperament, always stands a little aside anyway to observe any culture that she's part of. . . . [To be an observer is] a natural role, so it's not an anguish to be in it. . . . It's probably not entirely desirable to be integrated."[29] That said, Johnson does believe that transplanted Americans "become something else; that is, they become Americans with a slightly broader perspective. . . . In that sense I consider that I'm placed advantageously to see both America and Europe with a certain amount of detachment."[30] She draws once again upon the example of James to justify her status as, at once, "an American novelist" and "an international novelist": "James is the person who best reflects this. Most of his books did not take place in America, and yet we think of him as an American novelist."[31]

By chance the publication of Johnson's Franco-American trilogy coincided with the appearance of a number of other novels by American writers interested in France, including, for example, Claire Messud's *The Last Life* (1999), Edmund White's *The Married Man* (2000), and Monique Truong's *The Book of Salt* (2003), among many others. In June 2003, when Shakespeare & Company, the English-language bookstore in Paris, sponsored "Lost, Beat and New: Three Generations of Parisian Literary Tradition," its first literary festival in honor of what had become a discernable literary trend, Johnson hosted the closing-night reception in her Saint-Germain apartment. Her role as what might be considered the patron of the festival suggests a presence and importance within a contemporary community of Americans writing in Paris that is strongly reminiscent of Gertrude Stein. Whenever possible Johnson is present at the readings of American writers in Paris regularly organized by the Village Voice, another English-language bookstore.

In other respects, however, Johnson stands apart from the novelists of her generation. Her preference for the social over the individual, the cultural over the psychological, the analytical over the introspective, the observed over the confessed, and the ironic over the straightforward distinguishes her from many of her contemporaries. Although she reads four to five books a week

and admires many of her colleagues, including some that might appear surprising—Alice Adams, Alison Lurie, Susan Sontag, and Joan Didion but also
E. L. Doctorow, Don DeLillo, D. M. Thomas, Donald Barthelme, and even
Alain Robbe-Grillet—she does not read a lot of contemporary fiction, especially when she is writing. Rather she favors political and historical books or
books that she has already read.[32] Similarly, despite her strong interest in the
formal qualities of her own fiction and her stated sympathy for experimental
writing, she is not tempted to experiment in this way herself: "I am very sympathetic to experimental writing; it just doesn't seem right for me. I still
believe that I have a certain obligation to readability and suspense. From the
point of view of writing, I find it more interesting to take a situation and pro-
long it, which is, I suppose *plotting* in the old sense."[33] Like the displaced midwesterners or Californians in her novels, she too appears to remember "an
orderly society from which subsequent events have seemed to depart" and
shares her protagonists' "longing for that earlier orderly world."[34]

CHAPTER 2

The Southern California Novels
Fair Game, Loving Hands at Home, Burning

Prior to its publication in 1965, *Fair Game* was responsible for the only two letters of rejection that Diane Johnson ever received. The number of rejection letters is unusually small for an unpublished novelist, particularly one who did not even have an agent at the time, and their content was not only encouraging but also led to an exchange that is revealing about the problems of interpretation that all readers of her fiction face. One editor questioned whether the novel's characters were worthy of the attention they receive and advised Johnson to devote herself to a story she took more seriously.[1] Her response offers an intriguingly concise—and appropriately ambivalent—explanation of the dilemma confronting a writer of comic novels of manners: "The impression of underseriousness is a defect in my writing which I am trying to correct without spoiling what is good about it."[2] What is most satisfying about Johnson's writing, including *Fair Game*, stems precisely from the delicate balance she maintains between appearance and reality and from the subtlety and ambiguity of her ironic treatment of her characters. The other editor gave her the name of a literary agent who suggested that the novel might work better as a play. Johnson's bemused response, wondering "how you go about writing a play," no doubt serves as an example of her humor, but the suggestion itself also points to the important role she assigns to dialogue in the presentation of her fictional characters.[3]

The few reviews that *Fair Game* received predictably presented Johnson as a writer whose primary interests are regional and female-specific. The original cover blurb, for example, refers to "a sophisticated Southern California comedy" devoted to the subject of "sex and the modern girl."[4] In reality Johnson's first novel already demonstrates a broad interest in cultural diversity both within and beyond America, and a more accurate description of its content would be "sex and the eternal man." *Fair Game* begins in Tijuana, Mexico, where the first four chapters are set, and introduces readers immediately to one of the four male characters from whose third-person perspectives the entire story will be told. The opening sentence also illustrates the characteristically engaging beginnings of Johnson's novels: "Parker Peterson had read *Ferdinand the Bull* as a child and Ernest Hemingway as a young man, but he found himself poorly prepared for a genuine bullfight."[5] Parker's disappointment at the absence of "beautiful ladies in lace mantillas casting roses upon the matador" and his boredom at what appears to be "a dress rehearsal among actors who had never met before" also offer an immediate snapshot of the romanticism and the disengagement that sum up his character (3).

The initial setting of *Fair Game* illustrates the important role that place, both conceptually and specifically, plays in Johnson's fiction. Tijuana functions as a metaphorical crossroads where the paths of all the novel's main characters intersect in the course of a single day. Parker, who has abandoned poetry and graduate school in favor of public relations, is accompanied by his friend Marcus Stein, a Freudian psychiatrist with serious sexual hang-ups. Marcus introduces him to Emerson Kado, a famously eccentric writer whose own passion for bullfighting and Spain implicitly reference Hemingway once again. Seated behind Parker is the plain but persistently flirtatious Phyllis Hemley, whom he superstitiously fears he is destined to marry. In his effort to avoid her, Parker runs into his colleague Charles Earse, who is desperate to avoid him. The upright and moralistic Charles is embarrassed to be seen with his beautiful fiancée and lover, Dabney Wilhelm, with whom Parker promptly falls in love at first sight. Dabney, the successful author of a children's story, wanders off to meet Kado, who turns out to be staying at the same hotel, and to write her first letter to the poet Sam Trager; Charles meanwhile is busy lying about his whereabouts to his adored mother, the only important character other than Trager who is not physically present in Mexico. When everyone dines at the same restaurant, Marcus is introduced to Dabney, whom he finds irritatingly resistant to his charms, and Phyllis and Kado finally meet, to their mutual disinterest, in Parker's car on the drive home. It is, as one reviewer put it, "*La Ronde* American style" or, in the words of another, "an uninterrupted . . . maypole dance."[6] In ironic contrast to "Dynamic Space," the clearly misnamed American company for whom the passive Parker, the conventional Charles, and the predictable Phyllis all work, Johnson creates a figurative "dynamic space" outside the United States in which to unite her characters.

Parker, the first in a long series of outside observers in Johnson's fiction, functions more as a commentator on the action of the novel than a participant in it. Paradoxically, in keeping with the incongruity in which comedy often originates in the novelist's work, the freshness of Parker's viewpoint comes not from his naïveté or his foreignness, as is the case with such eighteenth-century prototypes of the model as Voltaire's Candide or Montesquieu's Persian travelers, but rather from his perfect adaptability: "Parker was always pleased to have an effect, any effect, on anyone, a thing he felt seldom happened. He liked to consider himself a misfit in the space world where he worked, in the academic world he had left, and even in the outside world, but he had secretly to recognize that being a misfit was not his real problem. His real problem was that he was a fit. He fitted everywhere, blended into his surroundings like a chameleon; he was a case of perfect adaptation. Wherever he went, people were glad to see him, but they were never surprised. They seemed to think he had been there right along" (15).

Although Parker distinguishes himself from his companions by his desire to experience Mexico as foreign, his vision is clouded, as in the case of the bullfight, by clichés of popular culture. The one authentic Mexican he meets looks "as if he might have played Porthos in a silent screen version of *The Three Musketeers*" (12), and he even compares the Tijuana prison he is unexpectedly obliged to visit to "the jail in Western movies about Texas" (48). Other characters are satirized as versions of the xenophobic or ignorant American tourist. The fastidious Charles, horrified by "all the stupid-looking and dirty people" at the bullfight (18), is relieved to discover that the hotel he has booked appears to be "a perfectly respectable place, quite American, in fact, with a few self-consciously Mexican touches" (21). Marcus, on the other hand, delights in the local color: he comes to Tijuana to purchase prostitutes and drugs. Only Dabney recognizes and relishes the foreignness she senses in the "strange land" of Mexico (35) and considers her "one night on foreign soil" to be an essential prelude to her plan to be "a world traveler" (21). As a result she is the only person in *Fair Game* who understands the paradox of national identity and the first character in Johnson's work to express one of the key insights that the novelist has explored throughout her career: "it is curious to find that one goes on being the same self in strange lands" (35–36). Part of Dabney's attraction to Kado, who is half-Japanese, lies in "the sincerity of his Japanization" (66), embodied in the style and decor of both his person and his property, which will serve as the geographical center of the exotic in the rest of the novel.

In contrast to Johnson's later work, *Fair Game* is a novel that privileges character over plot, at once in the literal, the literary, and the ethical senses of the word *character*. In its focus on both morality and relationships, particularly those involving love, sex, and marriage, it is very much a comedy of manners. Not surprisingly in the case of a first novel, the subject matter, tone, and narrative technique of *Fair Game* all reflect to some degree the influence of the nineteenth-century Victorian novelists whom Johnson had read and reread since childhood and whose works informed her graduate training and the academic career on which she was about to engage in 1965. Unlike many first novels, however, *Fair Game* is not significantly autobiographical. In keeping with the concerns of the novel of manners, the dilemma facing Dabney, forced to choose between a career and marriage and motherhood, is less a reflection of Johnson's personal life than of the general situation of American women at the time. Notably *The Feminine Mystique*, Betty Friedan's highly influential study of the societal values and pressures that led women to give up meaningful work and attempt to find their identity through the lives of their husbands and children, was published in 1963.[7]

Although there is no question of Friedan's direct influence, *Fair Game* raises, albeit humorously, many of the same questions that led to a national debate and the rise of second-wave feminism in the 1960s. The conventional Charles is the primary focus of Johnson's satire. His naive repetition of unexamined assumptions about female destiny is amusing in its exaggeration and its relentlessness, but what really makes Charles a comic figure is his conviction that he knows better than any woman "what a woman's real needs are. I mean, you can't deny that the family is a woman's main job. That's just biology" (105). The irony, which informs the reader's pleasure, stems from the fact that Charles is so often and so thoroughly wrong in his judgment of the women around him. To take one significant example, when he awakens from a nap in his Tijuana hotel, he sees Dabney, just back from her meeting with Kado and lost in reflection about her future as a writer, "in just the attitude he loved best, of seeming to wait only for him. . . . She was the picture of a beautiful wife" (31). As becomes evident in the course of the novel, Charles is even more dramatically mistaken about his own mother. His description of a fragile, demanding woman, in need of her son's protection and desirous to see him choose a suitably "Junior League" wife, is pure fantasy, a projection of his own outdated standard of femininity (80).

In the attention that *Fair Game* devotes to the act of writing, Johnson's first novel does resemble the early fiction of a number of first-time authors. Almost all of the central figures in the novel's multiple cast of characters are writers, a status largely relegated to secondary characters in Johnson's subsequent works. Indeed to the extent that Dabney, who also designs and sells children's clothing, is perfectly content to close her shop to honor Charles's views of marriage but reluctant to give up her writing, she may reflect Johnson's own belief that writing serves as a useful "cottage industry" for young mothers and housewives.[8] The nature of the satire in *Fair Game,* however, also suggests a parallel with more contemporary, even postmodern, works of fiction, which challenge the respect automatically accorded to literature and the literary community. Dabney is the author of *Mister Wister's Clock,* a children's story that has been comically overinterpreted by reviewers and critics as a brilliant metaphysical disquisition on the nature of time. Kado, for example, praises her "avant-garde fable" (28) as "a delicately constructed metaphor for the condition of being alive" (68); and Marcus lauds the genius of using a device as trite as clocks to "illustrate the utter insignificance of time" (96). When Dabney protests his reading, he dismisses the author as a mere "vehicle" who should never attempt to interpret her (or his) own work. In the absence of the actual story and the presence of inflated acclamation and contradictory interpretations, however, the reader is quite likely to trust Dabney's insistence that "it was intended for children" and to view the professional readings through her ironic eyes as confirmation that "it fails on that level" (35).

No one is eager to admit to having read the works of Emerson Kado, although most of the characters in *Fair Game,* including Charles's mother, appear to have done so, and everyone wants to know the famous writer. Kado, whose scandalous reputation recalls that of Henry Miller, is the author of presumably pornographic works that are banned in the United States and have to be smuggled in from France. Best known for "his youthful style of creative obscenity," Kado's very name has become an adjective: "Kadoesque prose" describes "a certain type of dark, strong, lurid writing" (26). Yet, however "secure" Kado's "position in American letters" may be, he is in reality a tragicomic caricature of the literary genius, famous for being famous, who has been unable to write for years (26). The charade he adopts of the great work eternally in progress recalls the second half of Dashiell Hammett's life, perhaps coincidentally anticipating Johnson's 1983 biography of him.

Kado's creative impotence does not prevent him from having his own personal biographer as well, one Mr. Spoon, whose name and faithful recording of the mundane details of Kado's daily life suggest a clear reference to the epitaphs of the dead that make up Edgar Lee Master's *Spoon River Anthology* (1915). Perhaps because the middle-aged graduate student has undertaken the project not only out of admiration but also out of self-interest, "in partial fulfillment of the requirements for the Ph.D. degree," Kado finds him an unsatisfactory partner for literary discussion, although he does read *Mister Wister's Clock* aloud to him in the hope it will "furnish one of the more endearing passages of the biography" (67–68). It is Dabney whom Kado seeks to turn into the protégée he merits as "one of the major satisfactions of fame and accomplishment" (30). However comical Kado's empty impersonation of the daring literary giant and however incongruous the contrast between his tiny, kimono-clad physique and the reputed enormity of his talent, he is nonetheless saved from complete caricature by the fact that he never stops worrying about why he cannot write and never gives up hope that he will again. Still Johnson does not miss a beat in her pastiche of a literary world that is seduced by personality rather than product and in which entertainment replaces substance, celebrity substitutes for achievement, and critics take the place of both readers and writers. In the final episode of the novel, one of Johnson's characteristic communal gatherings that bring her entire cast of characters on stage one final time, Mrs. Earse hosts a reception for Trager, "the Lenny Bernstein of letters" and current pretender to Kado's title of America's most important writer (295). They get on famously: "They stepped aside to become better acquainted, and, on the whole, Mr. Kado played so well his role of senior giant and aged mentor, and Sam Trager so perfectly was the glorious Alexander behaving with becoming deference to seniority and age, that the crowd collected all over again around the two of them and came away with the sense that it had heard a profound, a witty, even a historical exchange" (296).

Fair Game's parodic treatment of a culture of celebrity is further exemplified by Marcus's devotion to Kado. Although the young psychiatrist dreams of exchanging his respectable career for more adventurous endeavors, including "just possibly, writing," what he really wants is not to be Kado the writer but Kado the legend—or, at the very least, to play a starring role in its creation: "[He] would have liked at any rate to become the sort of itinerant great character real writers would meet up with in Alexandria and places and immortalize in their works. In short, he wanted to be the kind of character Mr. Kado had once been" (10). His actual purpose in Kado's life is to entertain and serve. The revelation of this information is illustrative of Johnson's comic effects, which are often attained at the sentence level by an unexpected transition that undermines the relative seriousness of what has come before: "Emerson Kado was fond of him. He amused Mr. Kado. He was an excellent talker on almost any subject. . . . *Also, he did errands in town for Mr. Kado*" (10–11; emphasis added).

Parker, whose youthful poetry was good enough to interest the famous writer, is so fundamentally apathetic and unmotivated that, having interpreted Kado's praise as a terrifying "obligation to produce, to improve, to try," he promptly fled to Dynamic Space, where he is ostensibly occupied with editing turgid scientific prose (11). Perpetually bored, he actually spends his days in ironic contemplation of the world and the people around him, as befits the narrator whose perspective is most often shared by the reader. What is comical about his character comes in part from the contrast between his state of permanent inertia and the vigorous mental activity required to maintain it: "Parker went to his office Monday morning and started out the day by taking pencils, several manuscripts, a technical manual, and a pair of scissors from his drawer. He arranged these carefully on his desk. Then he turned his back to them and lolled, peaceful as a water lily, adrift on the surface of his deep thoughts, resplendent in the sun of his finest resolution. Parker was content to sit all day doing nothing because he had resolved upon a course so positive, so active, that it virtually absolved him from any further work of any kind until the following February" (203). The passage above also illustrates Johnson's gift for creating extended metaphors that are at once poetic and admirably suited to the situation they describe.

Parker Peterson's favorite game, the alliteratively appropriate "Pertinent Platitudes," affords Johnson's readers a delightfully succinct version of the conventional values satirized in her first comedy of manners and a sharp contrast to her own clever writing. Although Parker cites them most frequently and most explicitly, well-worn clichés appear in epigrammatic form throughout the novel as justification for many of the characters' acts and observations. Parker draws on his personal collection of "the wisdom of the ages" in an attempt to resign himself to an inevitable future with the horrible Miss Henley (150). He finds particular comfort in the banal cliché that a bird in the hand is worth two in the bush: "It seemed, the more Parker considered it, that he was face to face with a Universal—either a Universal Truth or a lie universally propounded: a bird in the hand is worth two in the bush. Most people believed it, but it was perhaps only a matter of timid temperament. He examined his own temperament and sighed. It seemed like so much trouble to live a life of bush-beating, no matter how much one despised the bird at hand" (150–51).

Although Johnson ultimately opted for a different title for her first novel, the working title of the manuscript was "A Bird in the Hand." The original cover design, a curious image of finger puppets with one female figure in the middle surrounded by four men, identified Dabney as the "bird" in question and the title as clearly ironic.[9] Dabney is not only the single writer in the book who is deeply committed to the actual work of writing ("It's the thing I do best. How could I not take it seriously?"); she is also the only character who refuses to be content with what she already has (105). Reference is made repeatedly to her energy, her desire, her disdain for timidity, and her appetite for life in distinct contrast to Parker's crippling passivity, Marcus's cynical self-interest, and Kado's creative paralysis. Moreover Dabney is the only writer in *Fair Game* whom the reader actually has an opportunity to read. Although Johnson followed her agent's advice and removed the full text of *Mister Wister's Clock* from the final version of the manuscript, the novel is punctuated by six charming and introspective letters that Dabney writes to Sam Trager. Each merits a chapter of it own and appears in italics to distinguish it from the surrounding text. Although the letters are not fictional, they include Dabney's version of two classic folktales and function within the novel to represent her point of view, just as the character of Mister Wister was originally meant to do.

Although the recommendation to take out *Mister Wister's Clocks* may well have been a good one, given the difficulty of producing a convincing masterpiece that lends itself to interpretation on many different levels, Johnson's agent counseled a second change that the novelist fortunately ignored. On the grounds that Dabney was so secondary to the men in the novel that it was hard to tell who was meant to be the central character, the agent believed that she needed to be made stronger, clearly missing the point.[10] In keeping with the customary significance of the titles of her novels, Dabney is fair game for each of the four men who profess to love her, just as all of the characters prove to be fair game for the novelist's wit and irony. When the first game described, the opening bullfight, does not seem remotely fair to Parker, who pities the bull and identifies with the horse, Marcus reassures him that it is simply "an elaborate metaphor for sex" (13). A similarly ironic analogy to the "game" of sex occurs in an episode that allows Johnson to include political satire in her comedy of manners. Marcus, whose profession of populist views essentially consists of sitting with "the people" on the sunny side of the bullring and having sex with women who do not shave their legs, is the featured speaker at a meeting of "FAIR," or "For American Interracial Marriage." As he explains to Parker, "The only going civil liberties group, really. I mean, the others all want people to love each other, or hire each other, or live next door to each other. FAIR suggests only that they screw each other. It's got a hell of a lot more chance" (206).

Because Dabney is predominantly seen only from the perspective of others, she is as elusive as the meaning of her short story and just as prone to be misinterpreted. In a self-reflexive passage that functions within the text to mirror the subject of the novel as a whole, Charles ponders the puzzle of his fiancée in a conversation with a friend, who proposes a number of possible interpretations, each attributed to a different imaginary figure. In theory the reader of *Fair Game* confronts much the same problem as Charles, who concludes that he "just can't decide which is the real Dabney" (199). Since any direct understanding of her must be gleaned primarily from what she says, the predominance of dialogue in the novel allows Johnson's readers to be unusually active participants in the interpretive task facing the male characters. At the time of its publication, Johnson described *Fair Game* as "a novel about illusion, the ways in which people see other people because of what they are themselves."[11] Each of the four men in the novel constructs an imaginary woman to conform to his own ideal, a pattern that Dabney publicly denounces in the final scene: "None of you loves me. You just want me to *be* something to you" (293). In her first novel, Johnson distinguishes herself from many other women writers of the 1960s and 1970s whose work privileges female protagonists and first-person female narrators by her focus on relationships rather than individuals and by her interest in exploring male as well as female consciousness. Original and prescient within the context of early second-wave feminism, *Fair Game* is essentially a satire of masculinity in which Johnson perceptively defines men's expectations for women as the fundamental problem faced by those who seek to free themselves from traditional female roles.

Much of the humor of the text comes from the parody of conventional male types: Parker, the romantic hero; Marcus, the callous seducer; Charles, the devoted husband; Kado, the wise mentor. Or so they would have the reader believe, since the reversal of traditional gender roles works to similar comic effect. Thus, like the heroine of a nineteenth-century novel, Parker, not Dabney, considers his future destiny as a conventional spouse to be predetermined and inescapable. His passivity, his naïveté, his gift for gossip, his very likability all serve to feminize his character. Similarly Charles, not Dabney, is deeply embarrassed by their premarital affair and desperately afraid it will damage his reputation: "'Sometimes,' Dabney observed with some acidity, 'I think I'll have to marry you for the sake of your honor'" (20). The young engineer is also seriously outmaneuvered by the manipulative and secretly hot-blooded Miss Henley, who skillfully adapts herself to his ideal of pure, domestic, subservient womanhood in order to marry him. In another reversal Marcus, not Dabney, falls in love when she unexpectedly agrees to sleep with him; she, in contrast, confirms the stereotypical male belief that sexual pleasure can exist apart from emotional engagement. Kado is supported not by his writing but by a series of wealthy wives, of whom the most recent is a metaphorical "madwoman in the attic" who does not know the place to which literature has relegated her. Emma regularly emerges from her "moldering Spanish mansion" to wreak havoc on her husband's life, and her final retreat to an institution leaves him without an income (65).

Dabney's climactic moment of self-realization and understanding of men is weakened for some feminist readers by what follows: her apparent decision to sacrifice her newfound independence to a potentially similar relationship with Trager. In the novel's closing pages, Kado, Parker, and Marcus ponder a photograph of the poet boarding a plane for Greece; although "the friend" who accompanies him is "partially obscured behind the hostess" and "seen in profile," for the men there can be no doubt: "It was plainly Dabney" (306). Marjorie Ryan praises what she interprets as "a composite satiric image of three defeated men" but is troubled by the implication that Dabney "seems still to be seeking her identity through rather than with a man," one, moreover, who "is very much in the foreground while Dabney stands modestly in the background."[12] Even if one rejects Johnson's appealing but rather unconvincing suggestion that the scene is "probably just a fantasy," it is important to recognize a significant difference in Dabney's relationship with Trager.[13] He is the single male character who not only has no voice in the novel but over whom Dabney has narrative control in the same way that the perceptions of the other male characters structure the reader's understanding of her. The reader knows Trager only through the attributes that Dabney's letters assign to him, and in this case there are no conflicting views to challenge the truth of her portrait. Moreover the writer and narrator may always be in the background in relation to the characters they create, particularly in works of satire, as in *Fair Game,* where it is clearly Dabney who is foregrounded in a novel related by four male characters. Indeed if she does get on the plane, in this first of many examples of open-ended conclusions in Johnson's fiction, then Dabney escapes, literally as well as metaphorically, from Kado, Marcus, Parker, and Charles.

Loving Hands at Home

Johnson's second novel, published in 1968, functions in many ways as a complement to her first literary work. *Loving Hands at Home* balances *Fair Game*'s focus on masculinity with a more direct exploration of femininity, offering fictional corroboration that the unhappiness of American women, what Friedan called "the problem without a name," was indeed a multifaceted puzzle. The first-person narrator of *Loving Hands at Home* tells her own story and that of several other important female characters as their male counterparts are relegated to largely secondary and representative roles. Johnson's heroine is now an ordinary wife and mother with no particular talents, accomplishments, or ambitions to counterbalance her growing dissatisfaction: Karen Fry, in other words, is what Dabney Wilhelm feared that she might become. Elizabeth Berridge describes Johnson's second novel as "unashamedly feminine in both approach and appeal," and *feminine* may be the word most often repeated in the very positive reviews that *Loving Hands at*

Home received.[14] There was, however, some tendency among reviewers to assume that it was Johnson's first novel, which inevitably limited their understanding of its originality both within her own body of work and among the growing number of "women's novels" that had begun to appear, several of which are typically mentioned or even reviewed in the same article. In contrast those critics who had read *Fair Game* noted an evolution not only in the greater complexity of her characters' emotional lives but also in her talent as a satirical writer.[15] If *Loving Hands at Home* can reasonably be considered Johnson's contribution to the consciousness-raising novel of the 1960s and 1970s, the irony and humor with which she approaches the reality of women's lives also set it apart from the predominantly serious and realistic works of other women writers of the period.

The title of the novel is unsurprisingly ironic, whether or not Johnson had in mind the fact that "Loving Hands" is the preferred name of any number of home care services, assisted living establishments, pet sitting businesses, and ministries devoted to fighting various societal evils. Karen's periodic desire to volunteer her time to similar worthy organizations, including, in particular, a hotel for abandoned cats, seems designed to remind readers that loving hands may be more prevalent outside of the home than within it. Although houses do become spaces that are key to the understanding of the novel's characters, any illusion that the most clearly symbolic of these, the residence of "Mother" and "Father" Fry, is a place of security and comfort, let alone love, already begins to fade with the first of the four Sunday dinners that structure the book. Attendance is required at the weekly family gatherings hosted by Karen's in-laws, and the earliest of these functions much like the list of names and attributes that introduce readers to the characters in a play before the first act begins.

The patriarch of the Mormon family is an economist, so "well-appointed" that his daughter-in-law speculates that he must have been endowed at birth "with perpetual care, like a California burial plot." That Karen also presents him as "almost the only person in the family I loved" clearly does not bode well for the rest of the cast.[16] Indeed Karen, who regards her relatives with the eyes of an alienated stranger, has a gift for the backhanded compliment. Thus her mother-in-law, a prime example of "pioneer womanhood" with an M.A. in home economics, is "a splendid cook" whose specialties run to "molded gelatin salads and the use of marshmallows" (16). Their successful sons include Karen's husband, Garth, a surgeon, and Mahroni, a lawyer and the father of seven children. His wife, Joan, glows with "the holy light of domestic martyrdom," though Karen suspects "a spontaneous combustion of grievances" may be piling up below the surface "like oily paint rags" (20). In contrast Patty, her second sister-in-law and the mother, like Karen, of only two children, has "the fiery exterior" of a gypsy but an "essentially squawlike nature" underneath (20). Her husband, Sebastian, presented as "a factotum, a general secretary-chauffeur, assistant, and companion to a rich heiress art collector named Paris Pratt," is obviously harder to pin down. Karen cannot decide if such an ill-defined and clearly dubious profession makes him "a failure or a black sheep," but it troubles his wife greatly (18). Karen herself, on the other hand, disturbs everyone in the family, who regard her as an interloper and a misfit. Not only is she neither a Mormon nor a Californian, but far more important, she is the epitome of "domestic incompetence" in a world where such a flaw is unforgivable: "Domestic accomplishments had for the Frys a mystical significance related to femininity and the life force. The hearth, cakes, the cradle are still viable symbols, and lurk like native gods in the breasts of women outwardly converted to the League of Women Voters, and in the breasts of their husbands, the disenfranchised priests of an older worship" (14).

Although the Frys engage in certain Mormon practices, which paradoxically add to both the authenticity and the humor of *Loving Hands at Home*, Mormonism functions most importantly as a foreign country in Johnson's second novel. In her fictional portrait, the Church of Latter-day Saints represents less a set of religious practices than a collection of cultural beliefs, whose adherents promote a conservative social doctrine of conventional gender roles, the separation of spheres, and, especially, traditional femininity. Despite the conviction of one reviewer that "they'll hate it in Salt Lake City," the Frys do not actually turn out to be very good Mormons, and most readers will readily grasp the metaphorical purpose to which the religion is put.[17] By locating a Mormon family in California rather than in Utah, where a Mormon classmate and her family befriended Johnson during her college years, she ironically transforms a setting best known for its cult of personal freedom and sexual license into a hotbed of conservative values and behaviors. Meanwhile the stereotypically staid and stable Midwest, where Karen was born and raised, undergoes a similar metamorphosis to become the nostalgic location of female rebellion and social disorder. This curious mixture of a Mormon-midwestern-Californian novel—turned upside down to boot—clearly complicates the desire to see Johnson as a regional writer.

The opening and closing chapters of the novel serve as prologue and coda and establish an important narrative framework for the actual events of the story. Like *Fair Game, Loving Hands at Home* begins with a sentence that captivates readers and immediately attracts them to the narrator: "On a Friday morning I went to apply for a job as a fortuneteller at Pacific Ocean Park"

(3). As faithfully as if she were actually employed, Karen searches the want ads or, as she would say, the "Wish ads," three mornings a week to find interesting work for which she subsequently applies (7). The excitement of the search provides Karen with a "secret life," and although she never actually takes a job, being offered one bestows a cost-free boost to her self-esteem: "Being hired is like being constantly proved, renewed" (4). Johnson's stylistic ability to create an appealing voice for Karen, which quickly reveals her flaws as well as her charm, is evident in the rest of the paragraph: "It looked funny in the rain, deserted, everything stopped, *so* you saw the rust and peeling paint, *and* became concerned for the structural soundness of the fun rides, *and* resolved not to let your children go on them, *and* intended to write a letter to the Los Angeles *Times* about it" (3; emphasis added). Like the syntax of the sentence itself, Karen's life is full of pertinent observations, insightful conclusions, and good intentions, all of which multiply exponentially as the actions they point toward are constantly deferred.

The novel as a whole provides an excellent illustration of Johnson's theory that narrative dynamic does not exist in either, nor even in both, of two sequential events but rather in the space between them. The example she uses of an impending fall is particularly pertinent to Karen's situation: what matters is not that someone climbs a ladder and someone else pulls it away; what matters is the emotion engendered by the knowledge that the ladder will inevitably fall.[18] In the first chapter of *Loving Hands at Home*, Karen literally falls, in this case off a motorcycle on which she has accepted a ride from one total stranger while leaving her two-year-old son with another. The "reckless pleasure" she feels results from "the illusion that your life is your own, and not encumbered by the liens upon it of others' affections, your children and your husband, your own terrors" (6). With comic understatement Karen realizes that "a pratfall" in the middle of a busy Los Angeles intersection is "too large a symbol to be overlooked," and for the first time she acknowledges that she is not happy despite the charmed life she appears to lead (7). Having first had an Alice in Wonderland experience, Karen now passes through a Sleeping Beauty stage. Between the end of the first chapter of the novel and the beginning of the final chapter, she lives in the in-between space characteristic of Johnson's heroines; she subsists in a kind of limbo, watching and waiting, perpetually in the process of running away without actually going anywhere.

Analogies between *Loving Hands at Home* and the plots of fairy tales are fully consistent with the novel as a whole. Karen's marriage to Garth is a Cinderella story, albeit one in which Prince Charming turns out to be more interested in removing organs and collecting cars than in the proverbial happy ending. For lack of a castle tower, Mother Fry locks Karen up in the music

room to hinder her escape. As no doubt befits a wealthy, elegant, and enigmatic figure who fascinates everyone around her, Paris Pratt is most explicitly
compared to imaginary beauties: she is the Queen in *Snow White* (109),
Dante Gabriel Rossetti's "Blessed Damozel" (109), a floating genie "uncorked
from a bottle" (31), and the lady with the unicorn in the medieval tapestry
(131). Allusions to literary works in general are frequent and often amusingly
suggestive in *Loving Hands at Home*. Sebastian, for example, who would like
nothing better than to jump ship himself, reads Joseph Conrad's *Lord Jim*
(1900) aloud to his wife, and Karen keeps Henry James's *The Bostonians*
(1886), his overtly feminist novel, permanently packed in anticipation of finding the courage to leave her husband. During one failed attempt, she meets an
old woman resembling "the Wife of Bath," who, like Chaucer's prototype,
delivers a rambling monologue counseling against the evils of men and marriage (167). This pattern of intertextual allusion becomes increasingly prominent and revelatory in Johnson's subsequent work.

More important, however, the narrator of *Loving Hands at Home* is herself actively engaged in an explicitly literary act of narration. She explores various possible emplotments of both her own life and those of others in an effort
to understand, to order, and to confer meaning on experience. That she is
good at storytelling becomes immediately evident in her first job interview.
Unexpectedly challenged to demonstrate her qualifications, she must tell the
fortune of the skeptical personnel director, a pudgy, forty-five-year-old
man with calloused hands who works with female high-school dropouts. If
the future she foresees—moderate exercise, continued gardening, a younger
woman secretly in love, and a small inheritance—is simply reasonably consistent with the available physical evidence, what he praises are not her detective
skills but rather her knowledge of standard plot structures and literary conventions, the power of persuasion of which stems precisely from their familiarity: "The convinced, expectant look faded sheepishly from his face, and he
grinned. 'Not too bad. Sex, money, and health. That's about the formula'" (4).

Karen knows that her "secret life" is not really a life at all but only part
of the "game" she plays of "being Alma" (7). In keeping with the meaning of
the name, Alma functions as the embodiment of Karen's soul, the nourishing
model for an alternative self, one whom "Garth's family would really have
hated" (9). Since Karen's childhood friend offers far more sustenance than
Mother Fry, her current "alma mater," ever could, it is wonderfully ironic that
the Book of Alma, directly quoted in *Loving Hands at Home*, includes a key
chapter of the *Book of Mormon* in which the eponymous male prophet puts
down rebellions: "I could hear Mother Fry lecturing on something and quot-
ing Mormon scripture: 'Behold, the ax is laid at the root of the tree; therefore

every tree that bringeth not forth good fruit shall be hewn down and cast into the fire.' I looked it up later: Chapter Five, verse fifty-two of the Book of Alma. I supposed she was talking of me" (73). Karen's own "Book of Alma" stars the "town bad girl" of Bede, Iowa, who entertains her shocked classmates at birthday parties with stories of her sexual adventures and gives Karen her first lesson in how to run away from home. Although she has not seen her in years, Karen measures her own behavior against an imaginary standard of courage, competence, self-assurance, and independence incarnated by the now mythic Alma: "If Alma had ridden a motorcycle she would not have fallen off" (9); "it would have made another person—Alma, say— laugh" (34); "I mistrusted [fate], and some people, like Alma, trust it perfectly" (77). Only when Karen chances to commit adultery does she momentarily become "as fully conscious, as purposeful as Alma," whom she imagines to be watching over her (133).

The character of Alma also provides Johnson with an unusual context for the social satire that is one characteristic of the comedy of manners. In keeping with the work of James and Edith Wharton and like her own *Fair Game,* most of her novels are set in the exclusive upper-middle-class world of people such as the Frys. In Karen's case, however, her flaws in the eyes of her in-laws include not only her domestic incompetence, her Midwest origins, and her Protestant upbringing, but also her inferior social class, still worrisomely evident in the "peroxide blond" of her hair (12). In contrast to Karen's Cinderella story, her mother-in-law reads her son's marriage as a socialist realist novel: "Garth was involved, by marrying me, in a heroic rehabilitation effort, like someone in a Russian novel" (12). As a child, however, Karen is saved from the social ostracism endured by Alma because her small, conservative, resolutely middle-class town has the good fortune to include not one but two families who represent "The Poor," divided between "the Shiftless Poor" of the Phelps and the "Deserving Poor" of the Coes. With pitch-perfect mockery of the condescension and hypocrisy of the community, Karen argues that incarnating the latter is the far more difficult task. The women who hire her mother to clean are careful to call her "Mrs. Coe"; Karen is welcomed at the birthday parties of the rich for lack of any black children to invite; a reputation for "Character" is arbitrarily conferred upon her; and she too is forbidden to play with "Little-Alma-She-Stinks" (8).

Johnson's decision to experiment with first-person narration in her second novel proves to be a logical and in many ways an advantageous choice, but it is also a potentially limiting one, especially for a writer of social satire. On the one hand, Karen's overdetermined failure to fit into the world of the Frys affords her the ironic perspective of the bewildered outsider. Because *Loving*

Hands at Home is primarily Karen's story, it is important for readers to experience the world through her alienated eyes and to identify with her equally bemused and amusing voice. Moreover what sometimes seems like extreme naïveté on Karen's part is not only consistent with her youth and her lack of real-life experience but also with the overall structure of the novel. At twenty-six Karen does indeed need to "grow up," although not in quite the way that Mother Fry would have her do, and the story of her self-development ultimately makes of *Loving Hands at Home* a female bildungsroman (46). At the same time, however, one of Karen's first discoveries, the realization that she is far from the only member of the Fry family to have a secret life, makes the use of the first person considerably more problematic.

Johnson's primary solution reflects her continued interest in masculinity. Karen's brother-in-law Sebastian, the only member of the Fry family to defend her inside the family circle and to befriend her outside it, is the single male figure in *Loving Hands at Home* to merit significant character development and an important role in the action. To the extent that Sebastian, who also shares Karen's restlessness and dissatisfaction, functions as her soul mate, the adult counterpart to Alma, it is logical that he serve as a second, and theoretically secondary, narrator. Initially Karen's knowledge of events at which she is not present is explicitly introduced by statements such as the following: "Sebastian has since told me" (23, 74). Characteristically, however, the chapters justified by such explanations include far too much detailed description and delve far too deeply into private thoughts and emotions to have been convincingly related to Karen, at least in the form in which she repeats them to the reader. The fiction of the first-person narrator is therefore already potentially awkward in the case of Sebastian and becomes even more so when Karen needs access to the private lives of other characters.

Although first-person narration becomes more skillful and more convincing in Johnson's later fiction, its relative artificiality in her second novel does serve to focus the reader's attention on a narrative technique that would otherwise simply play an effective—and therefore largely invisible—supporting role. Transitions between chapters, in which lexical and syntactical repetitions connect Karen's life to that of Sebastian, insist on their twinship. For example her conclusion that "it is better, really, not to think about love at all" is counterbalanced by his ongoing obsession: "[Sebastian] was thinking, as usual, about love" (104–5). At other times the fact that Johnson makes no attempt to explain how Karen came to know certain things successfully reinforces the reader's sense of her isolation and alienation, despite a certain degree of narrative implausibility. Paradoxically, moreover, the maintenance of an essentially lighthearted tone in *Loving Hands at Home* actually depends on the limitations of first-person narration, since those characters—Garth, Mahroni, and Patty—who are theoretically harmed by the "secret lives" of Karen, Joan, and Sebastian remain fundamentally unknown. Garth and Mahroni, in particular, are exaggerated comic characters, stereotypical male chauvinists for whom readers have no reason to feel any sympathy.

The discrepancy between appearance and reality, a key structuring device in the novel of manners, turns out to be unusually substantial in *Loving Hands at Home*. The seemingly dull and morally upright world of the Frys is actually a fertile breeding ground for excitement and illicit pleasure once "love, or, to make the conventional distinction, sex, entered the picture, and from then on took over," as it does so often in Johnson's fiction (84). Mormon customs—and particularly their perversion—serve on a number of occasions to reinforce humor in the novel. The obvious advantage of Mormonism to a comic satirist of manners lies not in the foreignness of its religious beliefs, which are in many ways similar to those of Judaism and Christianity, but rather in the strangeness of its cultural norms. That their peculiarity is repeatedly acknowledged within the text itself by members of the Fry family, who do not fit the stereotype, clearly gives Johnson's readers permission to laugh.

Even inflexible Mahroni concedes that the temple garment is a bit odd: "To an outsider, the religious significance of a suit of underwear is likely to seem obscure, even ludicrous," a probable reaction that is verified in the course of the novel (45). In practice the "protective fetish" also does not serve very well to ward off the evils of the world (136). Sebastian, a self-described "Jack Mormon" who smokes, drinks, and seldom wears garments, alters his behavior on the very morning that his enduring dream of making love to Paris Pratt unexpectedly comes true (75). Since Sebastian is a hopeless romantic whose fantasies "always [come] out like sentimental nineteenth-century novels" (107)—in another example of the importance of literary models in *Loving Hands at Home*—his unusual appearance suitably converts his maudlin profession of love into comic farce: "There he stood before the object of his passion, the beautiful pale naked lady trembling ardently in his arms, she who had filled his thoughts, informed his every erotic impulse for six years, in a baggy nylon suit with appliqués on nipple and crotch." Fortunately Paris plays her part. With "the unfailing poise of the true lady," she finds his costume promisingly arousing: "How exciting. . . . It adds something, brings out the Salome in a woman. It's like seducing John the Baptist" (144). Since Paris is neither Mormon nor religious, her jest confirms that what interests Johnson is the comedy inherent in the disjuncture between expectation and reality and not the critique of religion.

Joan, the paragon of perfect female fulfillment, has an unusually exciting secret life. Nothing about the woman, whose "size, perpetual pregnancy, placidity, and silence tempt a comparison with some domestic animal," suggests that her exterior conceals a femme fatale who regularly seduces repairmen (20). The humor of this surprising play on a conventional male fantasy, which is far more likely to inform a pornographic film than the story of a woman's liberation, is reinforced by Karen's discovery of Joan and the soft-water man in flagrante delicto in a parody of Freud's primal scene. Joan's first experience with illicit sex takes place in the course of an official Mormon mission call, during which she ironically converts not the potential recruit but the purpose of the visit itself. In the process she also revives a metaphorical version of plural marriage. The association between religious faith and sexual infidelity is fully, albeit comically, appropriate given that the latter provides Joan with the emotional peace and solace that is more typically sought in the former; apparently sex even has the divine power to produce miracles, since a lump in Joan's breast mysteriously disappears after her first transgression. She reasonably concludes that the whole experience has been highly beneficial: "That was all. Joanie Fry, respectable mother of seven, member of the P.T.A., Sunday-school teacher, mission visitor, cook, seamstress, handy man around the house, president of the young married group at the church, and Heart Sunday Volunteer, had taken up illicit sex as a way of making herself feel better, with no more compunction than about taking aspirin" (103).

The serial infidelity of the devoted mother of seven is nonetheless not an obvious target for comic treatment, particularly when Joan discovers that she is pregnant with her eighth child. Precisely because her imagined suicide should be sobering, given that such misfortunes really do take place in the world beyond the novel, the fact that it is more amusing than sad provides a good example of Johnson's mastery of black humor. Readers are certainly likely to experience some discomfort at Joan's predicament. At the same time, however, the novelist's focus on her character's preoccupation with what in any other circumstances would be a minor and irrelevant detail transforms melodrama and potential tragedy into comedy. It is both absurd and perfectly logical that Joan should be unable to bear the limited number of colors in which toothbrushes are available: "The incident became central to her fantasy: mother of eight drowned in a nursery, and found floating in the wreckage with two red toothbrushes, one with a string tied to the handle" (204).

Knowledge of Joan's and Sebastian's secret lives confirms Karen's belief that every existence is arranged in accordance with archetypes or "great master plots" even as the surprising nature of those lives challenges her assumption that she has interpreted her own story correctly: "I had conceived of my life as conforming to one of the great favorite master plots—rags to riches. The poor and timid girl who manages, because of the triumphant collusion of personal merit and circumstance, to marry a prosperous and handsome man" (126). Although published ten years earlier, *Loving Hands at Home* could, with its striking similarity of vocabulary, be considered a fictional exploration of Hayden White's theory that individuals use story types to make sense of their own lives; by encoding experiential facts as a particular kind of plot structure or "Master Narrative," one endows them with culturally sanctioned meanings. Thus for White the choice of a life emplotment is always ideologically determined.[19] Johnson's novel suggests that she would not disagree with White, but she is also clearly aware that a traditional ideology of gender roles seriously limited the choices available to women in the 1960s. Not only does the archetype initially selected by Karen make this point, but so too does Joan's struggle to repress her hatred of her husband because the "great personal sacrifice" required to act on her revulsion is simply too overwhelming (156). That both Joan and Patty ultimately obey Mother Fry's injunction that no woman is "allowed to walk out on this life" highlights the difficulty and thus the courageousness of Karen's final escape (221).

When Paris tells the narrator that she "look[s] like someone who has left her self at home," the metaphor provides an accurate description of the absence she senses in Karen of any clear sense of identity, though the reference to home is also ironic in the context of the novel (125). Karen's path toward rewriting the story of her own self requires that she first confront the reality of "being Alma." When she calls Bede, Iowa, to learn the details of a life she imagines to be full of travel, adventure, and excitement, she discovers a plot at once more realistic and more fantastic. If most readers could predict that the "town bad girl" would return home with two children and no husband to take a job as "some sort of waitress," her death at twenty-four from an allergic reaction to penicillin is comically absurd (181). Karen compensates for the "loss" of Alma by narrating a very different story she claims to have heard from a famous French diplomat, who fell in love in Paris with the mistress of a European movie director, "a beautiful woman named Alma" (181). That Karen succeeds in convincing her listener that the story is true may have less to do with her determination "to do something for Alma, to make it all right" than with her incorporation of every cliché imaginable of the "master plot" of the Harlequin romance (181). Indeed Karen's story of Alma seems to conform to the same formula of "sex, money, health" that she draws upon to get a job as a fortune-teller in the opening chapter of the novel.

In reality, however, Karen's loss of illusions prepares her to take responsibility for the narrative of her own life and to begin to write that story as something other than either romantic fiction or domestic realism. She has learned, as all Johnson's female characters must, that life patterns are chosen, not preordained, and that personal identity is created, not imposed. In the final chapter of *Loving Hands at Home,* Karen and her children are no longer living at home. Although some may find the conclusion to Johnson's second novel as disappointingly open-ended as the first, Karen, unlike Dabney, has left, rather than left *with,* the hero. Although she is still living on the beach in what might appear to be an ongoing state of suspension, the final sentences assure the reader that Karen's situation has evolved and that it is temporary: "No, I am not running, nor am I waiting. I am reorganizing. The good weather will not last much longer" (232). Significantly the coda to the novel is the only chapter written in the present tense, which reinforces the sense of a future still to come, and it does not take place in any of the falsely named "homes" whose domestic space has imprisoned Karen up to now. The beach, which she describes as "a beautiful but enigmatic poem whose interpretation depends upon the erudition of the reader" (152), functions as a clean slate on which she can begin to inscribe a life and a self of and on her own. In the last pages of the novel, Karen builds a "fairy-tale" castle and then an entire walled city out of sand. In a fitting final metaphor, the woman does not inhabit the castle; she constructs it, and it does not belong to Prince Charming but to her. Karen has "regained [her] virginity" (232). One assumes that the next "wish ad" she answers will make her dreams come true.

Burning

Burning, Johnson's third novel and the last of her works to be set in Los Angeles, is also the only one that can fairly be considered a regional novel. Unlike her other fiction, which is located "for convenience" wherever she happens to be living, Johnson made a deliberate choice in the case of *Burning:* "That's the only time the setting hasn't just been the result of the fact that you have to put a novel somewhere. . . . *Burning* is the one that's most California, but the others, although they are set in the West, could have been set anywhere."[20] As the most immediately evident meaning of the title reveals, *Burning* takes place on November 6, 1961, the date that marked the beginning of the Bel Air–Brentwood fire, famous not only because it was the most disastrous brush fire in the history of Southern California but also because it threatened one of the wealthiest residential communities in the United States. It forced a number of people Johnson knew well, including her own in-laws, to evacuate. Despite the novel's origins in both autobiography and reality, however, what "most California" might mean to a midwestern writer of comic novels is a question without a predictable or an obvious answer, as readers of Johnson's earlier novels might expect. In her intriguing review of *Burning*, Joyce Carol Oates describes a book that is paradoxically both "superficial" and "serious" and whose juxtaposition of "lightweight serio-comic episodes" with "ghastly possibilities" might seem to suggest that "two different people had written the novel."[21]

Certainly notions of doubles and of dual personalities are key to *Burning*, whose third-person narration combines the narrative strategies of *Fair Game* and *Loving Hands at Home* by privileging in alternation the viewpoints of Bingo Edwards and her husband, Barney. The new visibility of the impersonal voice of the author's textual representative also serves to position the reader at a greater distance from the characters than in Johnson's previous novels. Thus in the opening paragraphs of *Burning*, a generalized narrative persona announces the moment at which "the world must burst into flames" by painting an impressionistic landscape in starkly contrasting shades of brown and white: "The heat in September in Los Angeles turns everything brown. . . . Those who stay are oppressed by the pervasive brownness of the scorched hills enclosing the city, and the sea is muddy, taking color from the hot, smoggy air. The pastels of the stucco houses bleach in the fierce sun to violent white and appear like vibrant purple blotches before the eye that stares at them too long."[22] "The eye that stares" subsequently takes form in the shape of Bingo, who is gazing down the hillside into the backyard of their closest neighbors as the novel begins. Required by the fire department to cut down the high—and highly inflammable—hedge that surrounded their new home, Bingo and Barney now "stood, as it were, naked on their hilltop, very resentfully" (4). Ironically, as in this scene, it is actually Bingo who most frequently adopts the voyeuristic gaze she fears from others. The exposure of the Edwards's house, in contrast, opens it up to actual invasion in a world in which no one ever seems to knock before entering. The opening pages of the novel thus serve metaphorically to situate the reader of *Burning*, who is similarly positioned as a voyeur, the fascinated witness to a series of bizarre and disturbing revelations.

Appropriately given the novel's general focus on questions and confusions of identity, Bingo initially mistakes the woman she sees below for her neighbor Irene Harris. In reality Max Gartman, a drug addict and welfare mother, is only one of the many devoted patients of Hal Harris, a Beverly Hills psychiatrist reminiscent of Timothy Leary. Hal's therapeutic strategies consist of sex and psychedelic drugs, whose beneficial effects include freeing him to wander off to tend to the exotic "succulents" whose fleshy tissue interests him far more than that of his patients. Hal's only nourishment consists of orange juice and cream, leaving his pretty young wife to expend her housekeeping skills on endless redecorating and an affair with the designer of the moment. Max is actually married to another Hal, who shares both his name and his general physical appearance with the first. Also something of a scientist and a womanizer, Hal Gartman spends his time inventing curious gadgets "for which there has not yet been a widely recognized need" (71). Noel Fish, a drug dealer and ex-convict who has been exiled from Harris's presence for having planted marijuana in his backyard, nonetheless keeps showing up unexpectedly not only at the home of the Harrises but also at those of the Edwards and the Gartmans. Not surprisingly given the context and the climate of the novel, its cast of characters also features assorted government functionaries: social workers, policemen, FBI agents, and especially firemen. The handsome Geoffrey Nichols, for example, plays a starring role in "the sex lives of Bel Air housewives" and is last seen carrying off the scantily clad Irene in a reenactment of "a fire-department recruitment poster" (36, 230). It is the memorable sight of this particular "naked man" swimming in the Harris's pool that keeps drawing Bingo's attention to her neighbors' backyard (6).

In short Johnson's fear that *Burning* would be "dismissed as a book about kooks" seems at first glance to be well-grounded, especially since Bingo and Barney largely share this view of those around them.[23] Although the Edwards are themselves native Californians, their decidedly Middle American morality functions as an effective substitute for the midwestern origins that distance characters from their surroundings in Johnson's first two novels. From the metaphorical height of their lofty hilltop house, Barney and Bingo initially view a stereotypically West Coast culture of fads, drugs, sex, and crime as a fascinating but dangerously foreign world. Midway through the novel, Barney provides a self-reflexive summary of the fictional situation: "Cops, robbery suspects, loony psychiatrists, nude firemen, unfit mothers. Tomorrow he would build a colossal, eight-foot-high fence" (128). Still as Barney's and Bingo's very names suggest, Johnson's protagonists are as eccentric in their own way as any of the secondary characters. Bingo introduces herself as a remarkable person, albeit one whose virtues are unfortunately embedded within less attractive qualities, as reflected in the syntax of the passage: "*Except for being plain and a terrible housekeeper,* she was a perfect wife. Cooked beautifully, sewed, was infinitely erudite on all subjects, was witty *when she wasn't depressed*" (5; emphasis added). Although Barney prides himself on "having had the good sense to marry a clever woman instead of a pretty one" (8), he can only make love to his wife, who resembles a buzzard in his eyes and George Eliot in her own, by fantasizing that she is "very, very stupid" (21). Since Barney's self-congratulation already sounds a good deal like the lyrics of a popular song, it is not surprising to discover that his name reminds Hal Harris of "Barney Google with the goog-goog-googly eyes," the hit tune inspired by the hero of a long-running comic strip (33). Given the figurative meaning of the word *dog,* it seems reasonable to suspect that the origin of Bingo's name may be similarly informed by the children's song "Bingo Was His Name-O."[24]

In her third novel, Johnson's continuing interest in character often borders on caricature, and her exaggerated humor is more reminiscent of farce or theater of the absurd than comedy of manners. It is fitting that the reedited Plume paperback appeared in 1998 with a cover designed by Mary E. O'Boyle and executed by Nina Berkson, whose collaboration produced the covers of all of Johnson's subsequent fiction. This example of O'Boyle's and Berkson's pictorial caricatures features an excessively long-nosed woman staring down with interest at the exceptionally long torso of a nude man in a swimming pool while elongated flames pour out of a house on a hill in the background. The best illustration of the ludicrous, however, is provided by the first example in the author's work of a recurrent character. Joan Fry, the lascivious Mormon housewife of *Loving Hands at Home,* who tells Karen at the end of that novel that "psychiatry doesn't really change your behavior, you know—it just makes you understand why you do things" (230), resurfaces in *Burning* as one of Hal's most enthusiastic patients. To reinforce the reader's pleasure at the intertextual connection, Johnson has Hal imagine himself from the perspective of one of his favorite plants, which stretches up toward his "loving hands" just before Joan's own "succulent" body turns green in the reflected light of a strobe lamp and wraps him "in her smooth leaves to receive his moisture and his restorative, nourishing care" (48, 54).

Readers of *Burning* may reasonably agree with Oates that the novel's "outlandish, zany" characters are "totally unsympathetic" and even that its principal narrators are "tiresome," but it would be a mistake to concur that such effects are somehow unintentional or a sign of failure on the part of the novelist.[25] The general tendency of reviewers to lament what they see as Johnson's lack of compassion for her somewhat unappealing protagonists is clearly fully consistent with their portrayal. Unlike her first two novels, in which humor and satire are directed at the circumstances and characters surrounding Dabney Wilhelm and Karen Fry rather than at the heroines themselves, the larger questions that interest Johnson in *Burning* make Barney and Bingo something closer to puppets of the author than to independent beings with whom readers might identify. In contrast to the naive narrators and outside observers of her earlier fiction, who reflect certain formal strategies of Voltaire's tales, in this case it is the newly prominent voice of an authorial representative and the manipulation of characters for a moral purpose that best recall the work of the eighteenth-century French philosopher and satirist. Appropriately Barney's allusion to *Candide* in the final pages of the novel confers prominence on the last of the many intertextual references in *Burning:* "Cultivate your garden—was it Voltaire who said that?" (241). Although *Burning*'s concerns are more social and psychological than metaphysical, the influence of Franz Kafka's absurdist fiction is also evident. Kafka is one of the few modern writers whom Johnson read early and whom she includes among her favorite authors: "Kafka was very important to me—is very important to me—the sense of being totally surrounded by strange forces you can't control."[26] The spirit of Kafka may best illuminate Johnson's assertion that she "found Los Angeles scary" and wanted *Burning* "to be a scary novel."[27]

The Germanic figure of the doppelgänger or double is key to what is potentially frightening about Bingo and Barney, whose identity or sense of selfhood is seriously threatened in separate and alternating episodes in Johnson's novel. Bingo's personal journey begins when she agrees to drive Max home to stop the Child Welfare Department from taking the Gartman children into its custody. Bingo's sarcastic dismissal of Barney's objections to her good deed—"A wild adventure, driving my neighbor down to Santa Monica Boulevard. Fraught with thrills and danger"—turns out to be surprisingly accurate (45). From the beginning Bingo finds herself oddly attracted to Max's proposal that they change places: "Be me for a while. It's all arbitrary anyhow" (58). Although Max's suggestion is based on the assumption that the differences between a "junkie kleptomaniac unfit mother" and someone "nice and clean, with short hair and shoes on" will not only be evident to all but will work in her favor, the reader is already aware that the two women resemble each other, at least in generic terms (58). Given the beauty standards of Southern California, a "homely" woman and a "plain" one may well look a good deal alike, which would explain why Bingo can find "no sign of irony" in the eyes of the social worker who greets her as Max even though he knows Max well (119). Bingo immediately reacts to Max's filthy motel room as if her own bad housekeeping skills were somehow responsible: "Strangely, it affected her like her own messy house, with the same defeated and incongruous sense of personal unworthiness. . . . But, of course, this was not really her personal disorder. She kept reminding herself of that" (65). By the time Hal Gartman comes home to propose they he and Bingo have sex, the reader is almost surprised that she declines his invitation.

What Bingo initially sees as an amusing escapade is rapidly transformed into a nightmarish experience when she succeeds too well at "the business of becoming Max" (59). Once Bingo decides that it will be easier and more convincing to answer questions truthfully rather than trying to imagine how her evil twin might respond, her own fragile self disappears behind her assumed identity, or—more frighteningly—she comes to the ironic realization that she has apparently *been* Max all along. To her horror Bingo, "a perfectly normal woman," finds herself declared an unfit mother on the basis of her own psychological profile: "These people were not looking at Maxine Gartman; they were looking, disapproving and powerful, at her" (163, 160). To the extent that Bingo is accused of being cold and detached from her children, who "barely seem to know [her]," she is the comically innocent victim of her own deception. But readers know Bingo well enough by this point in the novel to predict the disturbing answers she gives on the emotional and stability tests that they take along with her. Bingo really does believe that feelings of anomie, inadequacy, isolation, suicide, hate, and fear are "the reasonable way to feel" (162). In a parodic perversion of Johnson's exploration of the double, when Bingo finally resorts to confessing that she is "someone else," the social workers and psychologists are thrilled to have diagnosed dissociative identity disorder: "'Yes, yes,' said someone to Bingo. 'Two personalities!' whispered someone else, aside, excitedly" (162).

Bingo, moreover, is also the dupe of her own reluctance to appear to be the person she thinks she actually is. A stereotypical California counterculture is only one target of Johnson's satire in *Burning*, which also critiques mainstream bourgeois values and exposes the illusions of those who hold them. The specific sense in which Johnson accepts the book as "a Los Angeles novel" is based on her view of the city's residents as "people creating certain terrible types of illusion . . . people [who] have their own different styles of illusory self-preservation."[28] One of the first social workers Bingo encounters uses himself as the model for a generic portrait of the conventional "square," whom he assumes to represent a lifestyle that someone like her would find an anathema. On the contrary Bingo's realization that she is "just like him" brings tears of embarrassment to her eyes. Mr. Perguez ironically concludes his long list of qualifications for "squareness" by revealing one of the novel's primary strategies: "All those things satirists satirize, we do!" (120). His categorization of "the dropouts, like you" and "the Martini drinkers . . . these Beverly Hills types" as equally deviant further foregrounds Bingo's total alienation and paralysis, trapped between two contradictory and similarly unacceptable versions of herself. It seems only appropriate that the incident that ignites "the great Bel Air fire" is noted in passing just as Bingo begins her journey back to the privileged world she has renounced and that, ironically, is about to go up in flames (168).

Bingo may deserve her largely self-inflicted emotional pain, but her experience also provides the occasion for a scathing satire of the social-welfare system, the first example in Johnson's work of serious institutional critique. If Bingo is initially a comic character, able to distract herself with fantasies of nude firemen, she soon surrenders to the crippling apathy that has deadened everyone around her. Her sojourn through endless waiting rooms and multiple interviews gradually drains her of purpose and indignation "as if her thoughts were being vacuumed off and her head filled with a docility-producing vapor. . . . Everyone else in the room sat breathing the same gas" (109). Although the novelist's explicit and unusually elaborate intertextual reference to Kafka's "Metamorphosis" occurs in the context of Max's description of the time she spent in jail, the feelings of the prisoner are clearly analogous to those of the welfare client: "[It's] Kafka. You think you're an insect, an indescribably horrible but peculiar sensation consisting of your skin hardening and bumps coming out on you like stumps of new appendages, feelers and legs and things, and your eyes becoming flat or migrating into your fingertips. And then you get an insect brain capable of receiving only the crudest sensations; for instance, you would feel it only if someone stepped on you and squashed you, which you constantly expect them to do" (129). In the next chapter of the novel, the reader finds Bingo engulfed in a characteristically Kafkaesque world in which modern individuals are first silenced and then crushed by dehumanizing bureaucracy: "Bingo wondered whether, if she raised it, her voice would be heard, but she had no voice. She also had no thoughts" (137). Given that Johnson generally includes children in her fiction only for reasons of verisimilitude and almost never gives them any dialogue, her choice in *Burning* to make Max's children both visible and vocal strengthens her critique of a cruel system that willfully infantilizes its defenseless patrons.

The personal journey taken by Barney, a surgeon who is home recovering from an injured leg, is in many ways analogous to Bingo's, although it is also a more farcical counterpart. As is characteristic of the genre of satire, Johnson uses what Arthur Pollard describes as a "strategy of accumulation" to reinforce meaning by combining altered circumstances and characters with thematic and situational repetition.[29] In Bingo's absence "Who will take care of me?" is Barney's selfish concern, until Max miraculously appears before him for that express purpose: "I thought I'd come take care of you" (72–73). As the reader might expect, Max's impersonation of Bingo is much less serious and successful than is Bingo's of her, and it ultimately threatens not her own but Barney's sense of self. Initially when Max's friend Nelly shows up at his front door with a stolen Jacuzzi they are determined to test in his bathroom, Barney tries to convince himself that he might be able to rise to the occasion: "He had the makings of an adventure here, very possibly an orgy, a rare and unduplicable experience which, although he wouldn't seek it out, he oughtn't to miss if it offered itself" (83). In a stylistic effect that is typical of Johnson's language in *Burning,* a string of synonymous adjectives stresses just how unlikely it is that Barney will be able to overcome his identity as a "responsible, respectable, normal, nice, liberal" citizen, "the sort of person one knew," and indeed his "normative middle-class, middle-aged, middle-income inhibitions" fail to break down to release the "lascivious beast" he has briefly fancied to be hidden inside himself (80, 85).

Although the potential physiotherapeutic benefits of a Jacuzzi might actually help Barney, he quickly learns, to his increasing discomfort, that Max and Nelly are much more interested in psychotherapy or, to be more precise, in pop or pseudo psychology. Johnson parodies a stereotypical concern with the need "to find yourself" and to be "in touch with yourself" that is equally characteristic of the culture of Southern California and of 1970s America in general. Despite Barney's irate insistence to the contrary—"I *do* have a self"—Nelly's conclusion that he does not precipitates an identity crisis (105). To the extent that such a condition is most typical of adolescence, it perfectly suits Johnson's emotionally immature and ironically self-centered hero. When Barney suddenly announces that his "self" is what he does, the external narrator's aside openly mocks his conventionality: "as if no one had ever thought of this before" (106). Similarly Barney's need to end most of his sentences with exclamation points draws the reader's attention less to his anxiety than to his juvenile behavior: "I make things, then I can see them, and then when I understand their form better I understand me!" (106).

Barney is actually referring to his hobby as an amateur painter rather than to his profession. The studio he shows Max and Nelly is filled with dozens of oil paintings, all of which turn out to be self-portraits of the artist wearing a variety of curious costumes: "The room swam with faces, eyes. The faces wore funny hats, robes, masks. Some were green and contorted with malice; some melted into pastel beauties of irresolution. The face of a jester in his belled cap made mocking grimaces at the viewer. A Venetian gondolier regarded the ladies with tender, dark eyes and a musical, desirous smile" (113). These pictorial caricatures serve as an amusing metaphor for Johnson's general treatment of character in her third novel as well as a visual lampoon of the excessive narcissism associated with Southern California. The humorous effect is reinforced by the fact that Barney is every bit as ordinary looking as his wife. Although his paintings reflect his self-satisfied belief in the complexity of his own character, the sheer clutter of his studio is reminiscent of the fun-house mirrors of a carnival, which distort appearance and identity. Despite his earlier conviction that his art is the key to self-knowledge, when

Max asks which of the various depictions of clowns, bishops, mummies, and sheiks is "most" him, he realizes to his dismay that "the real corporeal Barney" may not exist at all (114). Although he lives a grotesque version of Bingo's experience, Barney finds that his metaphorical adventure ends in the same alarming absence of the self.

What in another context might be the chilling possibility of the literal destruction of the self occurs immediately after Barney's seriocomic discovery. It is "the ghastly reality" of the drug addicts Max and Noel injecting heroin that caused Oates to suggest that *Burning* was written by two different people. It would be more accurate to say that the novel pays tribute to a number of different writers. In the episode in question, for example, Max dates her drug problem back to her days as a beatnik, when she claims to have inspired Jack Kerouac: "I'm even in *On the Road* and a lot of other books about those times" (150). The passage also adds to the sheer accumulation of events that leads Barney to the remarkably understated conclusion—that it has not been "just the usual sort of day"—and Bingo to the doubly accurate observation that "it's been such a funny day" (236, 194). Virginia Woolf's *Mrs. Dalloway* serves as the primary model for the temporal concentration of Johnson's one-day novel. Her interest in exploring "the daily life" of Bingo and Barney, as filtered through their subjective thoughts and perceptions, is also reminiscent of Woolf's narrative technique.[30]

On the other hand, Johnson's use of the title image of *Burning* as a poetic device to unify and structure the novel probably owes more to Walter Pater, another English writer known for his prose style and his influence on early modernists such as Woolf: "What I wanted *Burning* to be about was people's private passions—their wish to burn, to generate heat, warmth, the Paterian phrase about burning with a hard gemlike flame and all of that. And how people's efforts to do that, or even to sustain a passionate commitment to life, are fraught with difficulties. . . . There's a lot of false fire around, a lot of stuff passing for emotional warmth and commitment that isn't really."[31] In the course of the novel, derivatives of the word *burn* appear frequently and in different contexts, referring to both literal and metaphorical fires: characters burn with sexual desire; faces and plants are scorched by the hot sun; people set things on fire or long to. Characteristically Bingo's fantasies of "lighting a match" to Max's messy apartment or burning down the firetrap where Children's Services are housed always end in the false fire of sexual fantasy (65). Although Barney uses the same Paterian phrase as Johnson to express his sense of "something that ought to be included in a life. Burning with a hard, gemlike flame" at the very moment that he and Bingo are finally reunited after their separate adventures, in this case, too, burning threatens to consume and destroy rather than warm or sustain (188). The physical separation of husband and wife throughout much of the novel figures a growing estrangement from each other that is consistent with their personal alienation from their own prior selves. Although the conclusion to *Burning* is characteristically open-ended, it is also unusually pessimistic. In the cheap motel where Bingo and Barney cling to each other as their home presumably burns, each pronounces in turn the final words of the novel: "Terrible, terrible. What will we do?" (244).

CHAPTER 3

The Northern California Novels
The Shadow Knows, Lying Low, Health and Happiness

The Shadow Knows, published in 1974, is the first of three novels set in Northern California. Although the change of fictional location corresponds to Johnson's own move to San Francisco in 1968, she wrote her fourth novel while on sabbatical leave in London and deliberately chose Sacramento over Los Angeles to challenge her emergent reputation as a regional novelist: "I decided after the reception of *Burning,* that Los Angeles was too loaded a place in the minds of readers, so I changed it to Sacramento. Nobody has ever complained about the Sacramentoness."[1] In an essay included in a collection devoted to West Coast writers, Elyse Blankley consecrates *The Shadow Knows* as the "*un-*Sacramento novel, a work that slips through regional parameters because, for the most part, it never sufficiently particularizes the landscape, history, and culture of Northern California."[2] But if the city itself is rarely identified and plays no relevant role in the reader's understanding of the novel's characters or events, place itself takes on a prominence and an importance that distinguishes *The Shadow Knows,* and the two books that follow, from Johnson's earlier work. These texts are located in generic spaces, conceived beyond specific spatial or temporal boundaries as broadly American. In this larger sense, however, the housing project in which the heroine and narrator of Johnson's fourth novel resides literally determines the action of the novel. The dominant mood of fear, the constant threat of violence, the ongoing reflection on the nature of evil, and the fundamental concern with race relations that pervade the novel all stem directly from its shadowy location within American culture and society.

    Initially the protagonist and first-person narrator of *The Shadow Knows,* identified only as "N." and "Mrs. Hexam," might seem to suggest what could have become of Karen Fry, the heroine of *Loving Hands at Home*, once her divorce was final. N. has also left home and is struggling to complete a graduate degree in linguistics and to support her four young children after a financially ruinous divorce from her husband, Gavin, a successful lawyer. If N. appears to be more decisive than Karen, who remains in a state of suspension at the conclusion of Johnson's second novel, she too is nonetheless stranded in the highly unstable space between her old life and a possible new one, which appears increasingly unattainable. *The Shadow Knows* unfolds during a one-week period, which extends from the day on which N. decides that someone is trying to kill her to the day on which she determines that the danger is over. In the interval Ev, the children's live-in caretaker, is attacked and dies; Andrew, N.'s married lover, breaks off their affair; and the family is subject to a series of acts of vandalism, which include slashed doors and tires, strangled cats left on the doorstep, and threatening pictures that arrive in the mail. Most of N.'s time is devoted to her efforts to identify the most likely would-be criminal from the many potential suspects, including Ev's predecessor, Osella; both her own and Ev's ex-husbands and past and present lovers; N's best friend, Bess; an unknown stranger; and even a phantom phone caller and an imaginary police inspector. That the dates in question, January 1–7, correspond to what is normally perceived to be an optimistic time of hope and renewal provides a key structural indication that Johnson retains her sense of irony and contradiction within the context of newly horrible and frightening events.

While *The Shadow Knows,* which was well and widely reviewed, redefined Johnson as an artist of national importance, its content might at first glance seem inevitably destined to reinforce her reputation as a writer primarily interested in women's lives and concerns. The superficial resemblances not only between Karen and N. but also between the two fictional women and Johnson herself might well add force to this interpretation, particularly in light of her own description of the book as "quite an autobiographical novel, probably my most autobiographical."[3] Like *Loving Hands at Home, The Shadow Knows* deals with the breakup of a marriage and the desperation of the mother of very small children: "That was really written from the heart, even though it was written when I was myself past that desperate stage."[4] To the extent that the novel is grounded in her personal experience, however, Johnson's principal interest nonetheless lies less in gender than in race. The focus of critics and reviewers on the narrator of *The Shadow Knows* led them to concentrate on the teller of the tale to the exclusion of the tale told, thus overlooking the essential fact that two of the three primary female characters in the novel are black. As Johnson has insisted, it is their story, not her own, that she and the narrator relate: "It wasn't in fact [N.'s] story—it was the story of the other women. Osella and Ev."[5] Both characters are based on women who cared for Johnson's children in circumstances identical to those described in the novel. In both fiction and reality, moreover, "Osella" has the same birthday, left-handedness, status as a former family retainer, obsession with witchcraft, and eventual descent into madness; and her successor, Ev, retains her real name in the novel.[6]

N. describes her neighbors as "blacks, and students, and welfare cases and just people who can't seem to manage things, the latter being our category."[7] Although Johnson selects N.'s dwelling precisely because a housing project is located at "the fringes of places where blacks and whites both live," within the framework of race and poverty, it is also remains very much a female, that is, a *human,* space.[8] In the several interviews from the early 1980s in which Johnson repeatedly rejects the labels of "feminist" or "women's" writer, she nonetheless also consistently argues that the traditional imagery of female domesticity is every bit as rich and as meaningful as that of the conventional male adventure; "the house," notably, is "as apt a metaphor for life as a ship."[9] Certainly this is the case with the geographically isolated living unit, which is structured in *The Shadow Knows* as a crossroads, a meeting place for those who are literally and figuratively out of place, an effect reinforced by the spatial unity of the novel. Since N. rarely leaves the apartment complex, which is at once a haven and an unsafe prison from which she cannot escape without a car, it is also the place to which every other character in the novel eventually comes, in a variant on the communal scenes that serve to unite the characters in Johnson's other novels.

Although Sandra M. Gilbert's review of Johnson's novel positions only its narrator within the general literary category of the woman who, by virtue of being abandoned, becomes "placeless" and "unaccommodated," the description more aptly suits Ev, who desperately wants "a place of her own," and Osella, whose residence is mysteriously undiscoverable once the Hexams force her to leave (28).[10] N., the fictional counterpart of Johnson, is fully conscious of the metaphorical significance of the house. Once Gavin moves out of their former home, she discovers that the roof, "that principal symbolic structure," leaks (103), and the "seedy façade" seems to expose the "seedy condition of [her] soul" to public view (111). In contrast the "well-preserved kitchen" of Andrew's wife provides a "useful and accurate symbol" of the hold that the fittingly named "Cookie" retains over her husband (124); the Masons move into a brand new home at the same time that N. and her children move to public housing. Significantly N. and Andrew first fall in love when the two couples take turns helping each other with home repairs. Thus the two lovers have literally "wrecked each other's houses" without regard for the inevitable consequence for the woman: "If she wrecked her home she would be homeless" (28, 30).

Johnson's favorite gendered analogy between the house and the ship may well have its origin in her childhood love of stories of sea voyages, of which the most famous adult version is Herman Melville's *Moby-Dick* (1851), a masculine tale in which another reflective and observant first-person narrator ponders the enigmatic nature of good and evil. Although the opening sentence of *The Shadow Knows* paraphrases a different textual precursor, discussed below, Johnson explicitly references Ishmael and Queequeg as models for her narrator's relationship with Ev, whose body is covered with scars that visually represent her destiny as an abused woman: "Ev is always cutting herself, burning herself, getting cut by others. . . . She has scars all over her, like dark lines. 'Evalin reminds me of Queequeg,' some friend of mine once said" (20). The reader's understanding of the friendship of Ev and N. as a parodic inversion of a stereotypical cross-racial male relationship is reinforced by the further recollection of Daniel Defoe's fictional autobiography of Robinson Crusoe and his companion, Friday: "Ev and I have been together about ten months but it seems longer, as it would to shipwrecked persons adrift together. We have become old friends" (102). Cast away with N. on a female version of a desert island, Ev saves her employer's life when she is the victim of an attack presumably meant for N., and it cannot be entirely coincidental that the "real, bitter blows" that lead to Ev's death are announced at the beginning of the "Friday" chapter (107).

Johnson's work typically originates in the effort to "capture some feeling of American life" that she finds oppressive, and what the editors of *A New Literary History of America* qualify in their massive 2009 reference work as "the persistent, though ever-changing issue of race" is unquestionably one of them.[11] Still her decision to write a novel about race relations, "about how things were between blacks and whites in the early 1970s," seems in retrospect, if not at the time, remarkably audacious.[12] Although it may well be the case that *The Shadow Knows* was read and reviewed by a predominantly white audience, Johnson was widely praised, in particular, for her realistic rendition of dialogue; L. E. Sissmann, for example, observed that "her conversations among blacks are the truest that any white novelist has done in years."[13] In keeping with the narrator's professional interest in language, the distinctive speech of the black characters, who include a number of men as well as Ev, Osella, and their female friends, is one of the primary ways in which this particular version of Johnson's novel of manners explores cultural differences. To cite only a single example, the following exchange takes place among Osella and her friends, who are baffled that her suitor Big Raider, whose arrival in the Hexams' lives introduces them to a "new experience of a black and white world," has not yet proposed marriage (114):

> Other times they would speak of Raider with cagey banter in their obscure metaphorical style.
> "When you gonna land that man, Osie?"
> "It ain't no man, Raider jus a peach, a big ole peach."
> "He done hung on that tree a mighty long time."
> "Well, he high up on the branches, mighty high up."
> "Heeee, heeeeee. The frost done got at him, you ask me."
> "Oh no, he been hangin there ripenin, but he was camoflagged.
> Now they done got me a 'lectronic ladder I'm gonna clamb up there and pick me that peach.
> "Heeee, heeeeee, hear the woman now. Wish her good luck!" (155)

Important to note in this passage is the fact that the women consider the house to be Osella's, not N.'s, and ignore the "little bitty woman" listening to them (155). In keeping with this transference, the success and originality of Johnson's exploration of race stems in large part from a fusion of identity that constructs Osella and Ev as what the novelist has called the "dark doubles" of the narrator.[14] Ev represents N.'s basic decency and courage but also her vulnerability and fundamental dependence on men, so that it is only after she is killed in N.'s place that Johnson's narrator gradually begins to take control of her own life. Osella, on the other hand, metaphorically kills N. herself. In contrast to Ev, Osella is more allegorical than realistic, a larger-than-life fantasy figure of Gothic and Victorian literature, an embodiment of the "madwoman in the attic" who finally—and ultimately quite literally—gets to take center stage in *The Shadow Knows*.[15] A symbol of N.'s repressed rage, Osella usurps her place with the children, including Gavin, whom she once raised, and takes revenge on her tiny rival by burning her in effigy. Still in Osella's last appearance in the novel as the central attraction at the Zanzibar, the seedy nightclub owned by Big Raider, N. is finally able to overcome her fear and identify with Osella as a powerful symbol of womanhood itself: "She seemed the embodiment of a principle . . . the female principle of which her body, grotesque and huge, was somehow the epitome and the supreme incarnation" (268). Similarly in choosing, out of all her possessions, to keep only Ev's diary, "an autobiography she was writing" that clearly corresponds to N.'s own narration, she again honors her common womanhood with a black woman and symbolically preserves both of their lives (190).

The close relationship of the three major female characters in *The Shadow Knows* allows Johnson to explore simultaneously both racism, including N.'s own, and its devastating social and psychological consequences for its victims. That the novelist's irony is primarily directed against her naive and self-centered narrator frees the reader to condemn attitudes and behavior related in an otherwise sympathetic voice. When she is cited for a traffic violation while driving with Osella, N. essentially blames her passenger for her personal humiliation and inconvenience: "If you have a black person with you, your white-lady immunity, which might entitle you to courtesy, is canceled, and the policeman will harass you as much as if you were black" (53). Similarly what should be N.'s outrage at the treatment of Ev, when she accompanies N. to a white retirement home, turns immediately personal: "I couldn't accept that a person could threaten *me,* and be undaunted by my superior social station and my womanhood and God knows, all because I was associated with black Ev" (209). In addition to illustrating the overt prejudice from which Ev and Osella suffer, Johnson's primary exposure of white privilege, the advantages that white people possess in a racist society, is both perceptive and strikingly innovative in any work, let alone a literary fiction written in the early 1970s about race relations in the United States.

Because the tragicomic novel of manners need not be straightforwardly realistic or openly political to produce its effects, the genre also allows Johnson to explore the destructive nature of clearly outmoded and exaggerated stereotypes, which, however false and absurd, permit N. to justify her exploitation of Osella by denying her not only individuality but also personhood: "She grins like a slave. Osella was a slave, and a slave was what I wanted" (33); "Around the house she was always smiling, had a bowl-full-of-jelly laugh, was the perfect jolly fat person. The perfect jolly darky" (51). Osella, who lives in a filthy room apart from the family, is indeed N.'s "madwoman in the attic," and her ultimate acknowledgment of her own complicity in a society that drives Osella into madness strikes the reader as accurate and just.

In the second of Johnson's novels, after *Loving Hands at Home,* to be related in the first person, the narrative technique is perfectly adapted to the story, in large part precisely because of the somewhat subordinate and ambiguous role assigned to N. The single initial by which she is identified points to her self-referential function as at once narrator and novelist. Her direct engagement with the reader, reinforced by the occasional use of the second-person pronoun *you,* beginning with the first word of the text, establishes an engaging conversational tone throughout the novel. The frequent passages composed of an extended string of questions work similarly to draw the reader into both the narrator's constant self-examination and the investigation of the incidents of vandalism and violence that surround her, just as the extensive reporting of dialogue positions the reader as each of the characters in turn with whom she interacts. The continuity of N.'s voice also serves as a primary structuring device for the narrative as she switches tenses from present to past to future to conditional and intermingles memories, daily reality, and imaginary occurrences. Her voice is so wonderfully personalized that readers have the impression that they can visualize N. even as they are at all times fully inside her mind; the strategy recalls the cinematic effect produced by the simultaneous use of a subjective camera and the mirrored reflection of the camera operator. N.'s gift for black comedy, self-deprecation, and tongue-in-check wit also accounts for much of the humor of the narrative. Thus, for example, N., who has been rather frivolously pondering suicide as a way out of her messy life, discovers that "waiting to be murdered" has paradoxically given her "something to live for," although she is still unclear about the expected decorum in such circumstances: "It's hard to have an attitude to murder because it hasn't happened to you before. You tend to think what a shame, what a shame it would be to be murdered; that would spoil everything" (6–7).

The representation of a character by an initial also suggests a parallel with one of Johnson's favorite writers. K., the hero of Franz Kafka's *The Trial,* also awaits death in a nightmarish world of uncertainty, trapped by unknown rules and unanswerable questions. The most common justification of first-person narration is to encourage identification between the reader and the narrator, and in *The Shadow Knows,* the reader is forced to share N.'s pervasive sense of fear, which dominates the text; the unnamed narrator could be anyone or everyone and, in particular, any and every reader. Because the mysterious events that occur convincingly explain the novel's overwhelming atmosphere of anxiety, suspicion, doubt, danger, and menace, Johnson was perplexed to find that some reviewers interpreted her narrator as paranoid, untrustworthy, and perhaps even insane. As she tells Janet Todd, who makes just such an assumption, "I had meant her to be a reliable narrator, and the events more or less real, and the fear certainly real. . . . so critical reaction, which was often to doubt or assume that the narrator was unbalanced in some way, surprised me a little."[16] In other contexts Johnson attributes such comments to gender bias: "I began to notice that female narrators, if they're of a sexual age, or a reproductive age, or an age to have affairs, aren't considered trustworthy. . . . I like to fly in the face of those prejudices and hope that I can make them authoritative and trustworthy reporters."[17]

In fact doubts about N.'s credibility may have far more to do with conventions of genre than with those of gender. The title of *The Shadow Knows* references the opening line of *The Detective Story Hour,* a popular radio show that premiered in 1930: "Who knows what evil lurks in the hearts of men? The Shadow knows!" Johnson's revision of the detective story begins with the first sentence of her own novel, where N., whose first-person narration makes her analogous to the mysterious Shadow, immediately reaches a very different conclusion: "You never know, that's all, there's no way of knowing" (3). The relentless crime fighter of the radio show evolves in Johnson's novel into the "Famous Inspector," whose imaginary conversations with N. focus on the interrogation of the victim rather than the investigation of the crime or the discovery of the criminal. Johnson's fourth novel marks in her mind the point at which she abandoned character in favor of plot as the major organizing principle of her fiction, a revision that led directly to her conscious engagement with questions of genre: "It is a kind of detective novel. I was intrigued with this form because I'm getting more interested in plot as I go along. I got tired of character, in fact, as a major consideration in planning my books. The detective novel seemed to be a genre which already existed, so it had a certain number of rules which specifically define the nature of its plot."[18] With characteristic irony, however, Johnson sets out in *The Shadow Knows* to expose the conventionality of the detective story and to deconstruct the traditional genre.

The novelist's description of the form, quoted above, is itself something of a comic understatement. The detective novel is not only the most highly regulated of literary genres, but it is also the only one that critics have repeatedly attempted to codify, as in the exemplary case of Ronald Knox's "Decalogue: The Ten Rules of (Golden Age) Detective Fiction" (1929) and S.S. Van Dine's "Twenty Rules for Writing Detective Stories" (1928). Unlike the many writers of formulaic fiction who willfully disobey some or all of the so-called rules and nonetheless produce convincing, satisfying, and recognizable versions of the genre, Johnson's metafictional exploration of the form is more in line with the postmodern mysteries of Paul Auster or the game playing of the French "New Novelists" Alain Robbe-Grillet and Claude Simon. In the first and final sections of the novel, N. foregrounds the textual sources that inform her reading of the world around her in an internal reflection of the text as a whole. From the beginning she is well aware that detective fiction is both strongly patterned and unrealistic: "For a while I gave up all reading but detective stories, whose sameness comforted me, whose morality assured me of order outside my own disorder" (36). Later when she is actively engaged in her own "detective game," she discovers that despite having "read all those detective stories, every one at the Elmwood Branch Library," she has no idea how to go about solving a crime (254).

It is not that the traditional elements—murder, motive, criminal, clues, detective, victim, even resolution—are missing in *The Shadow Knows*, but rather that they are excessively present and that their interrelationship is frequently contradictory and ambiguous. In Johnson's parodic and playful version of the detective novel, N., for example, is at various times both the intended victim and the perpetrator of the murder. In one possible scenario, "her life of crime" as an adulteress and a divorced woman merit death, and she inflicts it on herself: "A wanton woman is her own murderer, having first slain womanliness, delicacy, virtue, isn't that so?" (77, 79). Or else she is already dead, "killed" by the "death letter" her abandoning lover has sent her (7). Or perhaps she is guilty of having once fantasized about "murdering Gavvy," a plan she fails to carry out for the wrong reason—not, that is, because she turns out to be "an ordinary, sane, non-homicidal person" but because she "thought it wouldn't work" (130, 132). Or else her efforts to provoke a miscarriage have turned her into "a murderer" (5), in which case Andrew is the killer: "Desperate married man murders pregnant mistress" (130). At the same time, however, Gavin, who once hit her, informs an even more likely headline: "Estranged husband kills wife, children, self" (145). Throughout the novel N.'s rhetorical patterns—"maybe this and maybe that," "do and do not," "is or is not"—emphasize the proliferation of possibilities and the absence of certainty.

Despite particularly strong generic objections to the revelation that the detective is the criminal, at times N. suspects even the Famous Inspector, whose powers seem to include the ability to masquerade as her lover or her husband and, in one nightmarish fantasy, to incarnate both her "assailant" and her "rescuer" as they join together to murder her (87). The product of books or "old Basil Rathbone movies," N.'s imaginary detective is logically a parody of Sherlock Holmes, the stereotypical model of the aloof, intellectual, rational, superhuman detective, the exact opposite, that is, of Johnson's anxious, uncertain, emotional, and sympathetic narrator (4). N.'s ongoing conversation with the Famous Inspector serves as a confession and a self-examination of her flaws and failings. He is at once a psychiatrist, "a great student of human nature"; the priest who "instruct[s] his flock" at her funeral about the "perils of erotic self-indulgence and willfulness"; a "morally conservative" and humorless Victorian; and a relentless inquisitor (69, 93, 130). In all his disguises, however, he is so thoroughly insensitive and indifferent to N. and so obsessed with justifying her murder rather than preventing it that his persona paradoxically proves her innocent of all charges, if not in her own mind certainly in that of the reader. A real inspector, Dyce, shows up after Ev's death to make N.'s life even more dangerous and uncertain, if possible, and certainly more absurd. On the basis of her having once been arrested for drunk and disorderly conduct, Dyce, a more literal, pragmatic, and bureaucratic Famous Inspector, defines Ev, not her assailant, as the criminal. Moreover he finds it socially unwise even to attempt to investigate murders lest they turn out to be insoluble, which would prove "very demoralizing to the public morale" (203).

In a society in which even the police are "sympathetic to murder," clearly the famous conclusion to each episode of the serialized radio program, which assured its audience that "crime does not pay," is even more implausible than the question and answer with which the show opened (204). The dominant pattern of imagery within *The Shadow Knows* accurately reflects an uncertain world in which there is no fearless crime fighter to recognize and eradicate evil. The shadow that N. periodically glimpses lurking outside her home has evolved into a terrifying figure of random violence. In general the wide range of associations attached within the text to the title of the novel adds to its overall atmosphere of suspense and ambiguity. In a world in which all the suspects N. fears are treated by the police as "shadowy people" she might have invented (202), her final crisis finds her trapped in a Platonic cave in which illusion and reality at first appear to be indistinguishable: "I could imagine my room a cave now, myself a cave dweller forever made to look at the shadows of the real and I would never recognize the real when I saw it" (247). But once N. takes over the roles of both Dyce and the Famous Inspector and solves Ev's murder, an investigation that leads directly to her own rape by an unknown stranger, she realizes that shadows are always the reflection of something real. In the final paragraph of the novel, in which she has "taken on the thinness and the lightness of a shadow" of her former self, her metamorphosis is unexpectedly associated with a positive transformation into a more knowledgeable and confident human being: "I feel better. You can change; a person can change. . . . I mean your eyes can get used to the dark, that's all, and also if nothing else you can learn to look around you when you get out of your car in a dark garage" (277).

Not surprisingly the conclusion to Johnson's fourth novel was especially controversial. In keeping with the writer's tendency to paradox and irony, the ending of *The Shadow Knows* can look, depending on the reader, either too closed or too open, and once again both gender and genre are at issue. Johnson has repeatedly stated that despite her personal commitment to gender equality, she is not at all familiar with feminist theory, and at the time the novel was written, she could not have known Susan Brownmiller's pioneering work on sexual violence, *Against Our Will: Men, Women, and Rape,* published in 1975. Subsequently, however, when Johnson realized that some readers interpreted N.'s reaction to the rape to mean that she accepted the crime as a deserved punishment in which she was complicit, the author acknowledged in interviews and in her own review of Brownmiller's book that she would have ended the novel differently had she realized such a reading was possible: "I wrote that last scene lightly, before my consciousness was raised about the political implications of rape. I've had so much criticism about the scene, probably justified, and about having N. seeming to like being raped— which I didn't mean to imply at all . . . that I might now choose another metaphor."[19] Within the context of the novel, the violence against N., like the earlier assault on Ev, is a reassuring sign that the evil the narrator fears is not imaginary. The possibility that the danger N. and Ev face might involve rape rather than murder is periodically raised throughout *The Shadow Knows,* so the rejection of the misogynistic and judgmental Famous Inspector's desire to incriminate the victim can reasonably be taken to include this act of aggression as well.

As N. notes, one of the satisfactions of reading detective fiction lies in the certainty that order, if not justice, will be reestablished in the final pages. Johnson consciously chose to "make the mysteries proliferate" in *The Shadow Knows,* not only because she felt that such a parody of the formal perfection of the traditional detective novel would be "fictionally interesting," but also because she found such a structure to be a more accurate representation of the arbitrary and ambiguous nature of real life. She discovered, however, that the demand for closure may be the most exigent of the rules of popular fiction: "I've found that you don't tamper with conventions or that you *can't* tamper with them without creating a lot of reader irritation."[20] At the same time, however, the only responsibility of the novelist and her fictional double is to construct a coherent narrative within the context of an imagined world that may well remain deeply disordered, and in this metaphoric sense, Johnson, like N., finds the novel's conclusion to be satisfying and reassuring. Both view the enigmatic events that occur as "a series of almost unrelated mysteries, each needing to be cleared up," in contrast to those readers invested in the conventions of the genre who assumed a "connection, an unraveling of one ball of twine."[21] As an indirect but fortuitous consequence of Johnson's refusal to impose a conventional ending on *The Shadow Knows,* it becomes relatively effortless to respect the critical injunction to conceal the ending of a mystery, since in this case there is no traditional resolution to be inadvertently given away.[22]

Lying Low

Lying Low, which was nominated for the National Book Award for fiction in 1979, confirmed Johnson's reputation as one of the leading American novelists of her generation. The writer's fifth novel was more widely reviewed than any of her previous books, and for the first time it was clear that a number of critics, who compared *Lying Low* to *The Shadow Knows,* had begun to see her career in terms of a developing body of fiction rather than a series of discrete novels. Regional newspaper reporters, who tend to review four or five books in the same article, now consistently singled out Johnson's novel as the most interesting and praiseworthy of whatever group in which it was included. The *San Francisco Chronicle,* in a comprehensive biographical and critical overview by Grover Sales titled "A Lioness in Our Midst," presented her as the most prominent example of "Bay Area writers who are esteemed in New York's high literary circles, but who remain oddly anonymous and unsung in the old home town."[23] Although *Lying Low* happens to be set in Orris, California, and includes one episode that unfolds in San Francisco, the novel brings together a diverse group of representative characters who briefly interact in the unmistakably generic space of the boardinghouse, which one reviewer suggested could itself "be America."[24] Of all Johnson's works of fiction, her fifth novel is the one that best realizes her vision of America as a mythic and metaphoric place of cultural diversity and division, in keeping with David Fine and Paul Skenazy's description of literary California as "a kind of border crossing" for "a hybrid or a hyphenated population."[25] At the same time, however, *Lying Low* is also an important emblematic portrait of a 1970s America overtaken by violence, fear, and disillusionment.

Lying Low is even more tightly structured by temporal, spatial, and dramatic unity than is *The Shadow Knows.* Jane Mankiewicz began her review of Johnson's fifth novel by registering her amazement that the author "has sliced off four days and written a novel as disturbing but larger and riskier."[26] The action of *Lying Low,* in which all the characters are literally or metaphorically lying low, unfolds over the space of a four-day period, from the Wednesday on which a number of events are set in motion to the Saturday on which they reach what has come to seem their inevitable conclusion. On the first day, Marybeth Howe, aka Lynn Lord, who has been living underground since her involvement in a deadly antiwar bombing, is identified by Chuck Sweet, a high school classmate from Bettendorf, Iowa, and must decide whether to run or turn herself in to the police. Ouida Senza, a Brazilian immigrant who fears deportation since her official documents have been detained by a former employer, is planning a *festa* whose proceeds would allow her to buy back her passport and avoid marrying Mr. Griggs, her fifty-year-old sometime suitor. Theo Wait, who owns the house where the two young women are lodgers, is a sixty-year-old former ballerina and current dance teacher, whose devotion to liberal causes and local reputation as a do-gooder result in her reluctant agreement to participate in the arts festival at Fontana Prison. The fourth resident, Theo's brother Anton, is as transient as any other boarder; the noted nature photographer comes back to stay with his sister in between his failed marriages. By the end of the fourth day, plans to save Marybeth have come to fruition; Ouida's festival has ended in a destructive brawl; and Theo has been taken hostage and killed in an attempted prison break.

Although the plot may seem to suggest a novel of suspense, *Lying Low,* in keeping with its setting in the "Wait" House, is much more accurately described as a novel of *suspension.* In the strikingly effective and intricate opening section of the first chapter, the reader is introduced to Marybeth, who explicitly lives in a state of "suspended animation."[27] Her primary activity consists of looking out her window, and the early emphasis placed on an act that combines observation, passivity, and alienation establishes a pattern for the dominant narrative perspective of the novel: "From the upper window of an old house a young woman watches the postman on his daily rounds" (4).

Surprisingly given her actual status as a wanted felon, Marybeth makes her initial appearance as an enchanted princess trapped in her tower, a Sleeping Beauty or, from the point of view of the adoring postman, a "Rapunzel" (4). In the first example of the complex intertextual strategies that structure *Lying Low,* the former political radical will in fact evolve into a fairy tale heroine in the course of the novel. She will be recognized and rescued by the aptly named Chuck "Sweet," who, as the modern version of the archetypal prince, is simply the All-American boy next door:

> "I know," Marybeth said. "You're still the quarterback, aren't you?"
> "Yeah," he said. "Eagle Scout."
> "Head counselor," said Marybeth. "Alter boy. Class president."
> "Yeah, that's right," said Chuck. "Monitor. Honor camper." (184)

The unexpected lightness and humor of the passage above, and indeed of this particular storyline as a whole, clash not only with the overall tone of the novel but also with the actual destiny of former antiwar activists, whose eventual arrests and prison sentences are recited by Marybeth herself within the text. This discrepancy between fiction and reality is the first—and the only lighthearted—version of one of the primary interests of *Lying Low*: the curious combination of amnesia and nostalgia that marked America's relation to the 1960s in the following decade.

The beginning of the novel is actually related by a generalized third-person narrator, who sets the scene for events subsequently filtered almost exclusively through the individual consciousness of one of the three primary female characters. A theatrical metaphor is ideally suited to Johnson's evocation of a town and the daily lives of its citizens in a manner that inevitably recalls the role of the Stage Manager in an American classic, Thornton Wilder's *Our Town* (1938). The beautiful old homes on Ashby Path constitute an empty stage now that they have lost their original purpose; "too big for single families," they have been converted to impersonal rental lodgings that at present stand "vacant" in what will become an important fictional metaphor. Their curious architecture mixes genres and combines geographical regions in keeping with the stories and the origins of the characters who live in the only one that still has permanent residents: "nice gingerbread Victorian houses of Midwestern design" (3). The four central protagonists are introduced through the mail they do—or do not—receive: foreign letters and official summons from the U.S. government for Ouida; requests for charitable contributions and invitations to participate in arts festivals for Theo; multiple letters, reflective of his celebrity, for "Mr. Anton Wait" or "Mr. A. M. Wait" or "Antonw Ait," whom the postman assumes to be different people; and nothing for the girl "who gets no mail at all" (4). To the extent that the postal system suggests communication and connection and mail is delivered to people of known identity, Johnson's irony is immediately evident. The mysterious "termite man," who "carries a notebook in which he writes" and lurks behind trees to watch anyone approaching the house, seems to be at once a representative of the authorial narrator and a figure of both ambiguity and impending disaster (9). The abandonment of the politics of the previous decade in the wake of an evolution toward an increasingly insular and self-absorbed period of American history is also reflected in the changed neighborhood: "A decade ago, when Marybeth was a student, college slogans read 'Fuck War'; now they say 'Fuck Sacramento State'" (4).

In the sense that a "termite man" is primarily responsible for maintaining the structural integrity of a home, his role might also be said to parody one of the most important tasks of the novelist. Although the architectural foundation of *Lying Low* cannot be fully appreciated until the entire text has been read, its overall circular design is prepared and foregrounded before the novel proper even begins. The four sections named for days of the week are subdivided into twenty titled chapters, which are numbered sequentially throughout the entire work. From the beginning the chapter designations are clearly associated with irony given the discrepancy between the textual and intertextual references of the initial example: "Death in the Afternoon." Within the chapter "Freda Hen" is killed by "Mark the Labrador," and despite Theo's dismay at the death of "a most agreeable hen" and Ouida's ceremony to restore life, the "feathered corpse" is sent to the dinner table: "We might as well eat her" (11–13). Yet Theo's inexplicable reaction of apprehension, tension, and out-right fear—"Whence this fear—I'm not a fearful person, Theo thought"—suggests a closer connection to Ernest Hemingway's *Death in the Afternoon,* a history of Spanish bullfighting that also contemplates the nature of courage and fear (11).[28] At the end of *Lying Low,* the comic episode of a hen being killed by a neighborhood dog is tragically balanced by another "death in the afternoon," the demise of "the henwife" herself in a bomb explosion set off by a police blunder (13). That the explosives were made by aging hippies to help prisoners escape also makes Theo's destiny an ironic echo of the acciden-tal death of a scientist, killed during the bombing of a napalm lab by Mary-beth and her fellow student protesters. But what is most remarkable about the careful crafting of Johnson's fifth work of fiction occurs at the textual level where it began. In the final pages of the novel, readers encounter a self-reflexive observation that literally sends them back to the beginning of the text: "The old saying came to her: The ending is written in the first line" (268).

The expectations that Johnson sets up for the readers of *Lying Low* are somewhat more and differently demanding than those of her previous novels, but they also promise and deliver singular satisfactions. In keeping with the remarkable diversity of her body of work, the novelist followed the popular success of *The Shadow Knows,* whose plot-driven pacing, genre parody, and critique of racism and sexism significantly increased her readership, with the critical triumph of *Lying Low,* repeatedly praised for what Robert Towers, for example, in a widely quoted *New York Times* review, called "a nearly flaw-less performance—a beautifully constructed, elegantly written book."[29] John-son appears to have abstracted many of the same elements that accounted for the achievement of her fourth novel—mystery, crime, fear, death, suspense—and recombined them, on the model of Ouida's *feijoada,* to create something entirely new. Appropriately her clearest reflections on her interest in fictional form are explicitly motivated by the writing of *Lying Low.* In a 1983 inter-view, she notes that she makes a number of structural changes in the course of revision and then outlines how she goes about doing so: "If I had to place a priority on what really interests me, it would be on the *form* of a novel. . . . I usually work with outlines, and in these I work with formal principles of various kinds. I think of my books as having shape, as having parts which I move around. I even envision the process in a spatial way, in three dimensions somehow."[30]

In what the novelist also described as "a Virginia Woolfish novel of sensibilities of the seventies," her use of voice and point of view initially recalls the interior monologue characteristic of Woolf's fiction or the early work of James Joyce.[31] *Lying Low* is divided into fragments of varying lengths, each of which is filtered through the consciousness of a different character, as in the following example, which moves sequentially through the narrative perspectives of the three female protagonists as each makes her first appearance in the novel. The procedure is important enough to justify a quotation of some length:

> She watches out the window a lot. Unlike many criminals, she has had a happy childhood, so she can spend time thinking about that, or wishfully about men touching her breasts, or wondering whether Ouida will get mail. She has nothing else happy to occupy her mind. When she can get grass without too much trouble, she smokes it, too, on these long afternoons. . . .
>
> From her window, Marybeth has been watching Ouida walking slowly along Ashby Path carrying a big sack. A strange and horrid stench floats up from Ouida's sack as she sets it on the porch and fumbles for her keys. . . .
>
> Ouida carries her sack inside, down the hall to the kitchen. In the sack she has treasure. She's spent her life savings on this, the contents of this sack, big chunks of unsavory meat as dry as stones. She dumps them into the sink, hoping Miss Wait won't come in just yet.
>
> Miss Wait—Theo—notices crossly that the termite man is late and she wants to go out. But it is she who must await the termite man, because it is her house. . . . Theo hears the step on the porch and knows it can only be Ouida's, who is so heavy-footed. Theo has the thin person's impatience with the slow footsteps of the plump, the dancer's impatience with the stumbling. (5)

With remarkable economy the narrative establishes key traits of each woman, which will figure as recurrent motifs in the rest of the novel—Marybeth's boredom, arrested life, and sexual frustration; Ouida's timidity, determination, and cultural difference; Theo's social standing, ill humor, and intolerance of difference. Their practice of commenting on or attempting to interpret each other's actions adds to the complexity of the novel, as does the fact that each successive fragment furthers the overall development of events. The insistence on sensorial experience—sight, sound, smell, the suggestion of touch and taste—adds a lyrical quality again reminiscent of Woolf.

At the same time, however, as in poetry, the fragmentation of the narrative also creates a sense of discontinuity, reinforced by the blank space that separates each unified portion of the text from the next. This strategy serves as an ideal formal reflection of the content of *Lying Low,* whose characters are all solipsistic, alienated, and estranged from each other. Ouida's foreign customs seem odd to the Americans, and she has difficulty both understanding English and making herself understood; Marybeth no longer knows who she is and rarely speaks at all; garrulous Theo is trapped in her own memories and afraid of life; and Anton is a self-absorbed artist who by his own admission likes things much better than people. The periodic inclusion of intertexts within the novel further disrupts traditional coherence, particularly because the passages, quoted from whatever religious or philosophical text Ouida happens to be reading, are related, but only tangentially, both to the story that frames them and to the character looking over her shoulder.

On the one hand, this strategy is in keeping with Ouida herself, who is a human container for a curious mixture of contradictory beliefs gleaned from Brazilian superstition jumbled together with the ideas of different organized religions. On the other hand, the quasi-independence of the citations and the fact that they appear in a slightly smaller font than the surrounding print also foregrounds the autonomous existence of the text itself. This impression is reinforced by the periodic incorporation of ongoing reflections on a particular theme, of which Marybeth's extended rumination on "happiness" is only the most prominent (99–101). Interrupted by narrative events, such meditations recur in patterns that recall musical leitmotifs. The shifting tenses within *Lying Low* work similarly. Initially narrated in the present tense, a practice that continues to inform a number of individual fragments, the novel is also related in the past, so that the reappearance of the present becomes textually visible as well as narratively functional.

The creation of a textual collage or mosaic is consistent with Johnson's sense of her books as having a particular shape, composed of moveable parts, as if the novel itself were a kind of verbal puzzle. Such a metaphor is two-dimensional, whereas *Lying Low* realizes the novelist's complex vision of a three-dimensional fictional space. Like the anonymous narrator, the postman, the termite man, and Marybeth herself in the opening paragraphs of the novel, all of the characters are repeatedly described as fixed in an inexplicable but strangely durable state of watching and waiting. Theo's favorite hiding place on the stairway of the local co-op, from which she can observe everything below without being seen, is emblematic, but all of the characters watch each other from hidden vantage points, examine each other's mail, even enter each other's rooms when the occupant is absent. In keeping with their personal paranoia, Marybeth and Ouida believe that everyone they encounter is a potential government informant and that America itself is a vast network of secret agents spying on their fellow citizens. So eventually does Theo as well: "Perhaps they were being watched—detectives investigating them, wearing these disguises, meterman, postman, termite man" (185). Even Ouida's boyfriend, Mr. Griggs, is a uniformed watchman who repeatedly leaves her waiting indefinitely on street corners (47). Most important, the house itself appears to be waiting and watching: "'Everybody else seems to be waiting for something, too,' Anton remarked. 'Ouida and the girl. Stare out the windows . . . the house has the aspect of a brothel, a Middle Eastern brothel, watchers from the open windows, harem maybe, the watching faces of women'" (13).

Although a brothel, a meeting place for an eclectic clientele of strangers, is not unrelated to a boardinghouse, the female space of the Wait House is in reality both asexual and domestic. The only house on Ashby Path that is not vacant, it is nonetheless both literally and metaphorically defined as a vacuum. Denotation and connotation are at first amusingly fused by Ouida's inability to distinguish between the Portuguese *aspirador* and the English *aspiration*. The young woman's destiny is inscribed in this confusion, as her dream of an independent existence in America becomes steadily eroded by the inevitability of spending her life vacuuming Mr. Griggs's filthy carpet. Ouida also cleans endlessly at the boardinghouse, where the appliance casts a physical outline on the wall that she interprets figuratively as "the shadow of death" (113). The multisemantic symbol of the vacuum, combined with the emptiness of the house and the isolation of its inhabitants, creates a visual image of a three-dimensional structure that resembles a dollhouse with its facade removed. The reader looks at the house from outside, like the "strange watcher" who hides in the front yard or like the alienated Marybeth, who paradoxically imagines herself standing outside looking in on herself as if she were "a person viewed flatly through a window" (8–9). In this context the various events and subplots that intervene to delay the realization of the ending announced in the first sentence of the novel—Chuck and Marybeth's romance, a trip to San Francisco, Ouida's driving test, Theo's dance lessons—create the impression of looking into different rooms inside the house or of following visible paths leading in different directions within the architectural framework of the novel. The simultaneity of events involving different characters in different places increases the reader's awareness of separate planes intersecting.

In the same interview in which Johnson emphasizes the thoughtful attention she devotes to formal considerations in writing novels, she also states that she is "very sympathetic to experimental writing." Although she then goes on to propose that "it just doesn't seem right" for her, she immediately adds that she "wish[es] it did."[32] Although Tom Leclair and Larry McCaffery, the editors of the volume devoted to contemporary American novelists, include interviews with such postmodern writers as Robert Coover and Donald Barthelme, they also class Johnson among those that they deem "defenders of 'invisible art,'" writers who believe that language is inherently referential and narrative primarily a way to order experience.[33] If this characterization is generally valid, including to some extent for *Lying Low*, Johnson's fifth novel nonetheless also suggests that such a description is too limiting without careful qualification. In addition to the strategies of textual innovation described above, Johnson's fifth novel explicitly recalls the work of the French New Novelists and that of Alain Robbe-Grillet and Marguerite Duras in particular. Despite beginning a review of the latter's *The Lover* by observing that "Americans on the whole do not get on with the French novel and certainly not with the French experimental writers," Johnson has expressed her personal interest in Robbe-Grillet's fiction, and her *New York Times* review of Duras's novel, although it postdates the publication of *Lying Low* by many years, suggests a remarkable affinity with her work as well.[34]

The use of the present tense and the distanced point of view of the outside observer are particularly reminiscent both of Robbe-Grillet's early fiction and of the theoretical essays published in his *For A New Novel* (1963). His repetitive and apparently objective descriptions of places and objects, which actually serve to reveal the subjectivity of the novel's characters, are clearly akin to the narrative strategies of *Lying Low*. Critics frequently characterized Robbe-Grillet's prose as cinematic, and the pacing, presentness, and strongly visual quality of Johnson's writing merit this analogy as well. A circular structure, in which the end brings readers back to the beginning, is also prominent both in Alain Resnais's film *Last Year at Marienbad* (1961), for which Robbe-Grillet wrote the screenplay, and in *The Erasers* (1953), Robbe-Grillet's first novel. Johnson's practice of constructing her fiction according to "formal principles," which involve working with parts that she can move around, recalls Robbe-Grillet's procedure of structuring his novels according to the mathematically sequenced reappearance of particular motifs. Because Robbe-Grillet often alters chronology and moves between past and present, his fiction also functions as the verbal equivalent of a collage or a mosaic. All of the New Novelists used the device of the mise en abyme or self-reflexive inclusion within the novel of another artwork whose form and content mirror that of the text as a whole. *Lying Low* has the most prominent example of this strategy in Johnson's fiction and the one that is most similar to the New Novelists' preference for embedding a work of visual art. During a visit to San Francisco,

Marybeth unexpectedly comes across an exposition of Anton's photos, whose disturbing tone and images duplicate those of the novel as a whole: "On high white diagonal walls hung enormous photographs. . . . There were no people. Each was a composition of light and shadow; the menace of shadow elucidated the shining form" (109). The surprising number of allusions to various art forms within *Lying Low*—even Chuck Sweet is completing a Ph.D. in art history—foregrounds the formal precision and the attentive crafting of the novel.[35]

In their later work, the New Novelists went beyond autorepresentation to experiment with autogeneration, a textual practice that granted language a visibility beyond its referential function as a vehicle to convey meaning. Something similar occurs in *Lying Low*, where the connections among the characters function on a metaphoric rather than a realistic level so that the novel becomes a textual web interwoven by the repetition of particular ideas, motifs, and especially words. The most prominent of these involves a nucleus of meaning related to the notions of crime, murder, death, and prison, which will serve as illustration. Once the word *prison* appears in the novel, in the context of the arts festival at Fontana Prison, it spreads throughout the text, resurfacing in a surprising variety of different contexts (7). From the beginning, Theo's unease seems to be less for "the poor prisoners at Fontana" than "for all poor prisoners" (9). Marybeth wonders what kind of prison lies in her future: "She's afraid there is a special kind of prison, a kind of brothel prison. . . . She's afraid it will be a sewing prison, a broommaking prison" (156–57). Theo represents a much more terrifying possibility to the young woman: "thirty years of life imprisoned in your own meaningless head" (36). In a city bus passing on the street, Marybeth spots Ouida "in a whole busload of people like a prison van" (85); and Chuck, in his lovemaking, is "vigilant as a prison guard" (209). As a result of this semantic insistence, Theo's death, which is, as several reviewers pointed out, abrupt, unexpected, illogical, and unrealistic in terms of plot and character, nevertheless does not surprise the attentive reader. The language of death invades the novel to determine, indeed to overdetermine, the final explosion.

The fragmentation of the text in *Lying Low* and the impression that something mysterious but meaningful is happening in the silences and the blanks created by the textual gaps establish a clear parallel between Johnson's novel and Duras's work, as do the returning leitmotifs. Although the latter rejected the label of feminist writer, as does Johnson, Duras described the spaces and the voices of her texts as feminine, and Johnson's novel is similarly the domain of three female protagonists. It is the character of Theo, however, who will be particularly familiar to readers of Duras. Theo is haunted by memories of the past, the most meaningful of which she hints at throughout the text but reveals only at its end. An earlier recollection of a man dying in her hotel room in Finland functions, as is often the case in Duras's fiction, as a screen memory for the truly traumatic experience that Theo cannot forget. Her memory of the tragedy of a young girl falling overboard on an ocean liner stands out like an eerie foreshadowing of a virtually identical event that traumatizes the narrator of Duras's *The Lover*. In reviewing that novel as "a masterly balance between formalism and powerful emotional effect," Johnson might also be describing *Lying Low*.[36]

Despite Tuttleton's claim that the novel of manners has been ignored by contemporary critics because of their ideological commitment to avant-garde experimentalism, radical politics, or both, the genre is generally characterized by carefully patterned and well-constructed works of fiction.[37] *Lying Low* underscores the flexibility of the genre and confirms that neither formal experimentation nor the exploration of political beliefs is intrinsically antithetical to the study of manners. Johnson's fifth novel also introduces the comparative approach to the analysis of culture, an approach that has become increasingly important in her subsequent work. In what begins as an inter-American contrast between North America and South America, Ouida functions as a version of the naive visitor whose experiences in a foreign land inform a critical commentary on cultural difference. In this case, however, Ouida, whose fundamental goal is to understand and to integrate within American society, serves primarily as a target of American racial and cultural prejudice as the reactions of others expose their xenophobia. Although she is patterned on a stock comic figure in fiction, readers of *Lying Low* are likely to find her the one truly sympathetic character. Ouida is distinguished by her humanity and her optimism, and, in keeping with the general tone of the novel, her experience is more touching and poignant than humorous.

At the end of the novel, Ouida comes to an ironic conclusion about America's reputation as a cultural melting pot: "It is a joke on me that I spend much time trying to appear American and to be American in my speech and in every way, and now I discover that people treat me better when they think I am not American." Cynical Marybeth finds this realization paradoxical but unsurprising: "Americans don't mind foreigners, it's other Americans they're afraid of" (189). After the unanticipated narrative closure that the death of the main character seems to provide, Johnson characteristically expands the novel a final time to provide a satirical epilogue that inscribes a general, pervasive, and fundamental critique of American culture beyond any particular time or place. In a rambling monologue, Mr. Griggs delivers a long diatribe on injustice in America based on his experience with the Bank of America, the title of the final chapter. In the space of a few pages, his semisurrealistic narrative addresses racial prejudice, white privilege, social discrimination, white-collar crime, capitalist inequity, materialism, poverty, fraud, an unjust legal system, irresponsible lawsuits, and inadequate health care (267–77). The diversity of the problems he outlines thus provides a final glimpse into the complex and multitiered interior of Johnson's disturbing boardinghouse of a novel. Of all the writer's fiction, *Lying Low* is the one novel that seems to confirm her contention that she is at heart "a pessimistic person."[38]

Health and Happiness

Health and Happiness, published in 1990, is the last of Johnson's novels to be set in California and also the last of the eleven works of fiction that she has written so far to take place entirely in the United States.[39] As is the case with her two previous Northern California novels, Johnson chooses a generic space whose impersonality and cultural diversity make it the logical extension of the public housing unit of *The Shadow Knows* and the boardinghouse of *Lying Low.* This time, moreover, in contrast to the specific social and political context that informs the two previous novels, the temporal framework of *Health and Happiness* is as general as its physical location. The fictional Alta Buena, a modern San Francisco hospital, is fundamentally indistinguishable from similar health care facilities found in every city in the United States; and continuing concern about the quality and cost of health care in America makes Johnson's seventh novel as pertinent today as at the time it was written. The novelist herself has noted that the actual timing of its composition and publication was somewhat arbitrary: "In a way this book has been in my mind for years. I knew it would have to be written some day, and this was just the time for it."[40] Health and Happiness is the culmination of her longstanding interest, largely as a result of her husband's career, in medicine and medical ethics. The novel, described by Johnson as "stories brought home by John,"[41] is dedicated to her husband in an amusing disclaimer that exculpates him and his colleagues: "This book is dedicated to John Murray, who, however, should not be thought responsible for my viewpoint, and to my many other friends who are doctors, with affection and apologies."

Whether or not it is a result of its long gestation, *Health and Happiness,* despite its surface similarity to Johnson's previous novels, stands out as something of an anomaly within her developing body of work. The return to light-hearted comedy and overt satire clearly deviates from the expectations that some reviewers formed on the basis of the underlying seriousness of the social commentary and the innovative handling of genre and form that characterize *The Shadow Knows* and *Lying Low.* Although fear and death remain dominant motifs in *Health and Happiness,* they are now addressed with wit and optimism, so that reviewers appear to be simply offended by what they see as the novel's incongruity of place and tone, a reaction that is doubtless more revelatory of American cultural attitudes toward illness and hospitalization than of aesthetic preferences. Pearl K. Bell, for example, typically lamented "an unreflective novel about a subject that cries out for much more."[42] Although critics who alluded to hospital melodramas such as *General Hospital* or *St. Elsewhere* clearly meant such references to be pejorative, Johnson deliberately draws on popular culture to inform her humor, although she may have *Dr. Kildare* or *Ben Casey* more immediately in mind.[43] Philip Watts, Alta Buena's charismatic chief of staff, is introduced to readers as "most like a television doctor, serious, handsome, idealistic, formal, and irascible."[44] The exceptional popularity of television shows set in hospitals, a category recently illustrated by *ER* and *Grey's Anatomy,* may well contribute to the impression of ongoing relevance created by a novel published two decades ago.

The sense of a timeless classic, however, is also explained by the fact that *Health and Happiness* is a textbook example of the comedy of manners. Its title is borrowed from Oscar Wilde's *The Importance of Being Earnest* (1895), which David L. Hirst singles out in his critical study of the history and evolution of the comedy of manners for its exemplary influence on the genre.[45] Wilde's play, pertinently subtitled "A Trivial Comedy for Serious People," also provides the epigraph that announces the downfall of Johnson's male lead: "A high moral tone can hardly be said to conduce very much either to one's health or one's happiness." Dr. Watts, the only nonphilandering physician at Alta Buena and therefore a paragon of virtue and the self-proclaimed hospital moralist, will learn this lesson well when he falls in love with a patient, the beautiful Ivy Tarro. The title of *Health and Happiness* is also reminiscent of the alliterative pairings of faculties and feelings used by Jane Austen in *Sense and Sensibility* and *Pride and Prejudice.* Austen's novels in general, and the latter work in particular, are considered the cornerstones of the modern novel of manners. In the context of a story about adultery and marital discord, the fact that "health and happiness" also figure prominently in wedding toasts adds to the general irony that underlies the title.

In *The Novel of Manners in America,* a work designed to demonstrate the disputed importance of the genre within American fiction, Tuttleton provides a rare definition, and thus one well worth citing, of "a novel in which the manners, social customs, folkways, conventions, traditions, and mores of a given social group at a given time and place play a dominant role in the lives of fictional characters, exert control over their thought and behavior, and constitute a determinant upon the actions in which they are engaged, and in which these manners and customs are detailed realistically."[46] In the late-twentieth-century United States, the hospital may be the only remaining example of a hierarchical and rigidly structured society that is familiar and accessible to all citizens and that requires a complex process of accommodation for its successful integration. *Health and Happiness,* the realism of which stems from its technical accuracy and terminological correctness, verified by Johnson's husband, features a vast number of doctors, nurses, patients, and volunteers whose beliefs and behavior are fundamentally shaped by the ethos of the environment in which they work. The novelist's conception of the setting chosen for her seventh novel conforms with precision to Tuttleton's definition: "I was trying to write about hierarchy and all its rivalries. In a big, open society like ours, you can no longer write novels of manners—like Jane Austen's, let's say—in which the jokes or turns of plot depend on who is out of place. There is no place. But in hospitals there are ranks and social rules and you can tell a lot about your characters as they move within, and against, these structures."[47]

Despite a large cast of characters and a variety of individual perspectives that inform the novel's third-person narration, the hospital itself might most accurately be described as the main protagonist of *Health and Happiness,* a model that recalls, albeit in a very different register, Frederick Wiseman's documentary *Hospital* (1970). The novel opens with the general portrait of this protagonist, whose standing is immediately conveyed by its centrality within the city and its dominance within the neighborhood. From the outside the hospital's "fortresslike shape of reinforced concrete" suggests a prison; its decor, to which "every amenity of a modern interior environment . . . gives an air of a prosperous corporate headquarters," explicitly recalls the administrative center of a major company; and the hospital's public voice, which "speaks in the international accent of an airport page, with its reassuring intimations of ordered departures, safe returns," turns Alta Buena into a parodic airport terminal (3). In general the presentation of the hospital as an impersonal, international, anonymous, affluent space, indistinguishable from any other building of its kind anywhere else in the world, not only emphasizes its generic status but also makes it an exemplary postmodern place.[48] In a logical extension of the concept of "residency," all of the characters appear to live as well as work in the hospital. Several of them become metaphorically homeless in the course of the novel—Philip's wife exiles him, the intern Lum Wei-chi is thrown out of his sister's home, and, most revealingly, Mimi Franklin, coordinator of Volunteer Services, is harassed by hospital lawyers and staff alike until she agrees to move out of the house that lies in the way of Alta Buena's expansion plans. More generally the hospital is increasingly surrounded by those who are literally homeless, all of whom would "sooner or later . . . turn up at Alta Buena" (187).

Ironically Ivy Tarro's name appears to have predestined her for the role of the generic patient of *Health and Happiness:* "Ivy, kind of a pretty name, IV, intravenous" (35). Initially admitted to the hospital for treatment of a minor problem, she finds herself "tethered" to an IV for most of the novel once Dr. Bradford Evans, Philip's chief rival, misdiagnoses her swollen arm and prescribes the wrong medicine (21). In this traditional novel of manners, Ivy explicitly functions as the naive newcomer whose health and happiness depend upon her ability to adapt to the strange world around her. Initially frightened by her room, with its "various menacing implements for elimination" and television sets positioned "like surveillance units in a prison" (13), Ivy is soon desperate to please those on whom she now depends: "As weak as she was, she tried to smile at the doctor and nurse, so they wouldn't hurt her" (67). When she emerges from a coma, she has been thoroughly socialized; she directs not only "relief and gratitude" but also "tears of love" at her doctor for "paying attention to her" and "speaking so kindly" (121). In the course of her recovery, Ivy consciously sets about "learning hospital" as if it were a foreign language and culture; she eavesdrops in the hallways and listens in on doctors' rounds to master "the drama and the new vocabulary" (146). Her identification as the heroine of a novel of manners is reinforced by the strategy of repetition or "accumulation" common to the genre.[49] When Mimi is admitted to Alta Buena for acute pain of unknown origin, she too goes through the identical stages of terror, submission, observation, education, and integration. By the time Ivy is ready to be released from the hospital, however, her dependence has become something more akin to a comic addiction. Despite fulfilling the stereotypical fantasy of having sex with a doctor on the night before her release, Ivy's conclusion that she "loved the hospital" more accurately identifies her relationship with the true hero of the novel (139). When she reintegrates Alta Buena on the symbolic occasion of New Year's Eve, it is less a visit than a homecoming; she has already decided to apply to medical school.

The events of *Health and Happiness* unfold during the month of December, a time frame actually based on Philip's term of service in the rotating position of chief of staff but largely experienced by the reader as a reflection of Ivy's illness. Although there are clear indications of day and date early in the novel, once Ivy fully realizes the passive role inherent in her new identity as a patient, the reader loses all specific awareness of the duration of events, in keeping with Ivy's own "sense of being outside time" (120). As a result of the relative shortness of the chapters of *Health and Happiness,* one reviewer made the amusing suggestion that the novel as a whole "proceeds in slow drips," presumably like those of an IV.[50] The errors made in diagnosing and treating Ivy also determine the plot of the novel and turn it into a medical mystery. Although the resemblance is no doubt coincidental, in spite of Johnson's conscious intention to give her writing in *Health and Happiness* a "spare, journalistic quality" different from that of her previous fiction, this aspect of the novel resembles nothing so much as "Diagnosis," the fascinating column that appears in the *New York Times Magazine* each Sunday.[51] "Diagnosis" provides a detailed and highly dramatic account of a patient who presents unusual and often incompatible symptoms and whose condition inevitably worsens following his or her admission to a hospital. After batteries of tests and consultations with specialists and several incorrect diagnoses, the solution often turns out to be something banal that the doctors are embarrassed to have missed. Similarly, and in keeping with the conventions of the detective novel, readers of *Health and Happiness* are given a number of clues that Ivy's swollen arm is a minor complication of breast-feeding and that Mimi's sharp pain is the result of a simple bruise. Ivy does not sue her doctor for malpractice, nor presumably do the protagonists of "Diagnosis," but it seems interestingly appropriate that the *Times* column is often directly followed by another weekly feature titled "The Ethicist."

Alta Buena naturally has a medical ethicist on its staff, the rather disturbingly named Vivian Mudd, as well as more than seventy-five other characters identified by name. Curiously one of the primary criticisms of the novel focused on a lack of in-depth characterization, a complaint that is both accurate and completely irrelevant in an ensemble piece in which everyone's identity is determined by the function he or she performs within the vast social network of the hospital. Although the helplessness, innocence, and odd religious and medical beliefs of some of the patients inform a few humorous incidents, it is the hospital itself, rather than any particular individual within it, that figures as the target of satire in *Health and Happiness*. Johnson's novel explores the full range of passions, problems, and intrigues that make up the daily life of a modern health care institution—hostility between internists and surgeons, malpractice suits, incompetent doctors suing for reinstatement, fund-raising dinners, nurse's strikes, and residents on cocaine. As emotional mistakes and romantic misunderstandings multiply, the idea of misdiagnosis extends beyond the medical realm to structure the novel as a whole. Mimi, for example, repeatedly misinterprets the romantic intentions of both Dr. Evans and Dr. Watts, and the entire text is punctuated by the unpredictable and often outrageous consequences of Wei-chi's constant cultural confusion.

Alta Buena is also the source of overt comedy, extending at times into the realm of farce. Indeed the reader of *Health and Happiness* is treated to three lawyer jokes worthy of stand-up comedians. Philip's nemesis, MacGregor Bunting, aka "Mack the Knife," is far less concerned when the unscrubbed chief of staff invades an operating room to rescue Ivy from surgery already underway than when he learns that all the recipes submitted by surgeons have been excluded from the hospital cookbook edited by Philip's wife. In a parody of the bureaucratic nature of institutions, the hospital physicians spend significantly less time assisting patients than attending meetings of the Medical Journal Club, the Doctors' Parking and Advisory Committee, or the Morbidity and Mortality Conference—affectionately known as "M&M." Philip, the ironically inconsistent moral center of Johnson's comedy of manners, is obsessed with "medical etiquette" (56), "the rules" (57), "the simple protocol without which things would fall into chaos in a hospital" (124), and the "medical decorum" that stipulates that "doctors had to be perfect" (62). He also has sex with a partially paralyzed Ivy in his office in the middle of the night: "Short of amputating the wrong limb, it was the riskiest thing a person could do, courting the most horrendous consequences" (168). Even the holiday season figures into the playfulness of the novel. Philip is visited by one of the hospital's "three wise men," charged with watching over their colleagues for signs of stress or instability. Ivy encounters the Dickensian "ghosts of Christmas" as she ponders a major career change: "Now Christmas Future assumes the guise of a smart, white-coated technocrat, suavely showing her herself wearing a white coat, with a stethoscope in her pocket" (237).

Both Ivy's previous career as the maître d'hôtel of a trendy celebrity restaurant and the complex process of revising the hospital cookbook support the incongruous association of food and illness, which establishes the overall comic rhythm of *Health and Happiness*. Despite frequent allusions to the hospital's stereotypically "unspeakable" food, Alta Buena's many committees include the Hospital Gourmet Food & Wine Society (124), which organizes a fund-raising gala in honor of the novel's hero. Ivy's explanation of her background includes a direct reference to two possible interpretations of the novel's title: "I just thought food was interesting . . . the physiology of food, and the way it makes people *happy and healthy,* or *unhappy and unhealthy*" (141; emphasis added). She first sees her swollen arm as "a great white sausage," later revised to the more gastronomically correct "boudin blanc" (8, 22). After her unenthusiastic return to work, the comparison is reversed to correspond to her new interests: a berry pie leaks "bloodstains"; a lemon tart is "urine-colored" (231). The potentially grotesque juxtaposition of a culinary and a medical vocabulary clearly lends itself to black humor, and Alta Buena patients who go into a coma are welcomed to "the vegetable garden" (54). The "professional class system" of the hospital is respected in the cafeteria, which has separate dining rooms for nurses and doctors, whose senior members consume "huge quantities of caffeine, cholesterol, and fat," while their younger colleagues stick to the salad bar and Wei-chi eats prodigiously "as if permanently in mind of Chinese famine" (15). Philip normally appears outside the hospital only during his nightly dinners with his wife. In the course of the novel, Jennifer Watts moves from one food fad to the next, giving up in rapid succession red meat, all meat, shellfish, all fish, leavened bread, all bread, and so on. Her dilemma over whether it is ethically acceptable to continue to serve what she has decided not to eat makes Philip's dismissal from their home a promising first step toward his own personal health and happiness.

Despite the predominantly comical and satirical tone of the novel, *Health and Happiness* indirectly addresses serious concerns of both the sick and their caretakers, including fundamental issues of life and death that result from the ambiguous advances of modern medicine. Relatives who refuse to take permanently comatose family members off life support coexist with doctors who ignore the wishes of their patients and proceed to resuscitate and treat those who will never recover. If a miracle is perhaps inevitable during the holiday season, the one that occurs is highly ambivalent. In an event so contrary to medical predictions that it resembles "the outcome of a television drama," Randolph Lincoln awakens from a three-week coma in time to become Alta Buena's "poster boy" at the gala fund-raising dinner (151). In a particularly painful example of the contradiction between appearance and reality, a contrast that is traditionally a key element of the novel of manners, the promotional materials show "a handsome, strapping young man" when, in fact, Randall, who has suffered brain and liver damage and is dying from an incurable disease, is barely able to sit up or speak (156). In its vast inventory of events that are likely to take place in a hospital, *Health and Happiness* also includes an unmistakable, if paradoxical, act of heroism. What remains of the medicine that almost kills Ivy allows Philip to save the life of another young woman. Although many of Alta Buena's patients are preoccupied with their mortality, only the very old die, and in fact one of those whom the reader, like Ivy, believes to have passed away unexpectedly shows up in the intensive care unit at the end of the novel.

In contrast to other cultures, Americans are notoriously reluctant to face up to the reality of death, and despite its hospital setting, readers of a comedy of manners as frank as *Health and Happiness* are likely to expect that all will end well. For once Johnson does not disappoint them. The conclusion of the novel returns to the realm of popular culture, although romantic comedy now

appears to be a better analogy than serious medical drama. The novel's protagonists inevitably turn out to lead charmed lives in a world in which "nothing bad ever happens to doctors" (250). Ironically Philip not only receives the
award given annually to the most valuable faculty member, but he also discovers that the clearly unprofessional affair he expects to destroy his career
actually brings him not only sympathy but also increased respect: "For reasons he could not understand, so far from being an object of pity, unfairly vil-
ified, he has become once again the object of everyone's approval. Can it be
that there are those who can have their cake and eat it?" (252). His single
source of disappointment is likely to be the woman he adores. Unable to pay
her huge medical bills, Ivy realizes that the obvious solution is to choose her
specialty carefully, and she makes the most ironic choice possible in the context of the novel: "Surgery, she thought. Oh, definitely, surgery is the thing"
(260). *Health and Happiness* may mark the moment at which Johnson's' final
sentences become as entertaining as the opening sentences of her early novels.

CHAPTER 4

The Franco-American Trilogy
Le Divorce, Le Marriage, L'Affaire

As early as 1983, Diane Johnson conceptualized her interest in America within a comparative framework: "I want to write about Americans, and you can really see them better in the context of another society."[1] Ten years later circumstances provided the novelist with an unexpected but highly opportune occasion to explore the value of a cross-cultural perspective. Since 1994 Johnson and her husband have lived in Paris for six to eight months of each year. This move, originally motivated by Dr. Murray's ongoing work with international health organizations, has no doubt had a far more profound effect on her career than on his. In keeping with Johnson's practice of correlating her place of residence and the settings of her fiction, *Le Divorce* (1997), *Le Mariage* (2000), and *L'Affaire* (2003) all take place in France, primarily in Paris, and together her eighth, ninth, and tenth novels constitute what the writer has characterized as a Franco-American "trilogy."[2] In retrospect, moreover, the choice of Paris as both a real-life and an imaginary location seems less arbitrary than inevitable. As Johnson notes in *Into a Paris Quarter* (2005), the autobiographical text that complements her fictional trilogy, the French capital has long held a "special fascination" for American writers and a "significant place" in American literature.[3] If Henry James and Edith Wharton, two of the most prominent of Johnson's expatriate predecessors, are the undisputed masters of the novel of manners, it is surely in part because Europe, and especially France, also provides foreign writers with a model of what is more difficult to find in modern America: a society whose strong regulation by cultural norms and traditions makes it relatively difficult for outsiders to understand, let alone become integrated into. In Johnson's own words upon completing the trilogy: "It's easier to write a comedy of manners in a society where manners are important."[4]

The general epigraph to *Le Divorce* fittingly introduces the significance of national identity by citing James, whose international version of the novel of manners focuses on Americans abroad and contrasting Old and New World values: "Man isn't at all one, after all—it takes so much of him to be American, to be French, etc." During a six-month stay in Paris, Isabel Walker, the first-person narrator of the novel, experiences the complexities and conflicts of cultural difference and identity that have intrigued the novelist ever since Dabney Wilhelm made the curious discovery that "one goes on being the same self in strange lands" in *Fair Game,* Johnson's first novel.[5] The exceptional commercial and critical success of *Le Divorce,* a bestseller that brought Johnson her third National Book Award nomination in 1997, suggests that the now-classical story of an American falling in love in and with Paris continues to fascinate the reading public. In keeping with the Franco-American cognates that serve to title the three novels, their popularity was equally evident outside the United States, where all three works appeared almost simultaneously in French translation. *Le Divorce* was also the first of Johnson's works to be adapted for the movie screen. James Ivory, the director of the 2003 film version, is well known for his adaptations of novels of manners and particularly those of James, including the internationally themed *The Europeans* (1979) and *The Golden Bowl* (2001). Johnson's particular version of the cross-cultural romance has a long history in American cinema; *Une Américaine à Paris,* the title chosen for the French translation of *Le Divorce,* openly references *An American in Paris* (1951), the Vincent Minnelli musical that is the most famous of Ivory's Hollywood predecessors.

In the case of *Le Divorce,* moreover, the external meeting of fiction and film reflects an important internal strategy that serves to unify and structure Johnson's novel. The text begins with a three-page prologue in which the narrator, a film school dropout, introduces her story "as a sort of film."[6] Consistent with her family name, Isabel Walker takes the reader on a figurative *flânerie,* a form of strolling particular to the capital of France, immediately foregrounding the continued importance of place in Johnson's work and inaugurating a practice of fusing two competing cultures. The opening sequence, destined to appear "under the credits" (1), is constructed as a montage of characters and scenes that constitute the raw material whose subsequent rearrangement will engender the novel to come. Isabel begins with "an establishing shot from a high angle," which singles out the Eiffel Tower, the paradigmatic icon of France and the symbol of Paris. As suits the lightness and humor of Johnson's fiction, the metaphoric camera moves in to focus first on the "cliches of Frenchness—people carrying long baguettes of bread, old men wearing berets, women walking poodles" (1). At the same time, however, her narrator also prepares the reader for the realism and the accuracy of the novel's portrayal of French culture. Beyond the traditional stereotypes and the conventional tourist attractions exists the actuality of a modern metropolis: "those Art Nouveau entrances to the metro that seem to beckon to a nether region of vice and art but actually lead to an efficient transportation system" (1).

If such a paradox is potentially "a clue to the French themselves," cross-cultural irony is immediately evident in the "series of close shots" that challenge the accuracy of stereotypes by exposing the American origin of many of the people Isabel sees on the streets of Paris. At the same time, the visually objective "closeups of individual Americans," most of whom "might be mistaken for European," indicate that in a global world physical appearance no longer discloses nationality (1–2). The behavior that does—disgust at smokers, suspicion of high fat content, impatience with bureaucracy, and, of course, a "strong American accent" in speaking French—already announces key differences between the customs and values of France and America. In a continuation of the cinematic technique that underlies Johnson's postmodern practice of autogeneration, Isabel subsequently identifies those first presented as "generic Americans" as "some of the actual people in [her] story" (2). The establishment of "the cast of characters" of Le Divorce leads directly into a plot synopsis, whose focus on Isabel's sister Roxy, whom the narrator has come to Paris to help, contains the essential elements—adultery, divorce, finance, friendship—conventionally attributed to the novel of manners: "Her French husband has left her, she is about to give birth, and we have at stake a large sum of money" (2). A final look at the picture as a whole reveals that the landscape of the novel remains suitably haunted by several generations of literary expatriates: "There are, also, certain ghosts of Hemingway and Gertrude Stein, Janet Flanner, Fitzgerald, Edith Wharton, James Baldwin, James Jones—all of them here for something they could not find back home, possessed of an idea about culture and their intellectual heritage, conscious of a connection to Europe" (3).

The general structure of Le Divorce, which was composed after Johnson's most concentrated period of screenwriting and adaptation in the 1980s, further displays the lessons she learned from working in another genre. In addition to the privileging of plot over character, which is already evident in Health and Happiness, she began to conceive of her novels more episodically than in the past, on the model of the sequential images of the cinematic storyboard, and to imagine her own role as analogous to that of a film editor.[7] The creation of a narrative alter ego trained in film production justifies the foregrounding in *Le Divorce* of particular scenes, so designated, in which the staging directions and the dialogue follow the explicit format of a script, as in the following brief excerpt from one of many such examples:

Scene: Yves and Isabel in a restaurant that reeks of cigarette and cigar smoke. . . . Yves smoking like the rest.
ME: It's really stupid to smoke. It's the leading cause of death. Do you have to?
YVES: *Bah oeuieeagh.* . . .
ME (primly): I'll have the healthy fat-free sole and the steamed vegetable plate, please.
YVES: *Pavé au poivre, saignant* (thick steak, rare, dripping with butter and cream).
ME: Ugh (shudder). . . . (69–70)

Such passages, which recall the theatrical origins of the comedy of manners, frequently highlight the communal scenes that are also key to the genre. The cross-cultural conversations that take place inevitably expose, albeit humorously, significant differences between the customs of France and the United States. It is important that Isabel openly identifies film, which replaced theater as the world's favorite form of entertainment, not only as the genre on which her own story is patterned but also as the key to understanding Franco-American relations on both an individual and a societal level: "Film, with its fitful changefulness, its arbitrary notions of coherence, contrasting with the static solemnity of painting, might also be a more appropriate medium for rendering what seems to be happening, and emblematic too perhaps of our natures, Roxy's and mine, and the nature of the two societies, American and French" (4).

In reality it is indeed "the nature of the two societies" that constitutes the principal thematic interest of *Le Divorce*. In Johnson's particular interpretation of the familiar plot of the cross-cultural romance, whose implications are admirably summed up in Edmund White's perceptive dictum that "a love affair between foreigners is always as much about the mutual seduction of two cultures as a meeting between two people," the customs, beliefs, and behaviors represented within the novel ultimately matter far more than the individuals who temporarily embody them.[8] Johnson draws once again on the strategy of accumulation, characteristic of the satirical novel, to raise the trope of the Franco-American couple to the level of a generic model by multiplying its variants. Thus Roxy's French husband, Charles-Henri de Persand, leaves her for another European who is also married to an American. In addition to Isabel's doomed romance with Edgar de Persand, her brother-in-law's elderly uncle, she also has affairs with several young Frenchmen. In the background Charles-Henri's sister runs off to London with her English lover, and several other Franco-American couples of Roxy's acquaintance split up. By the end of the novel, Roxy is involved with another potential French husband, and Isabel's attraction to a second French politician promises to help her forget the first.

The close family connections of many of the novel's characters support the bemusing speculation, reinforced by the contrast between Francophile Roxy and her very American sister, that cross-cultural relationships are criminally incestuous, although the frequency of adultery provides an even more appropriate metaphor for the impure, "adulterated" mixture produced by the attempted merging of different cultures. It is hard to know if the cause of what seems to amount to high treason is the original union of spouses of different nationalities or their seemingly inevitable estrangement, but in requesting testimonials from French friends, Roxy has the impression she is "asking them to betray their country" (99). In *Le Divorce,* the titular act of which leads to violence and crime, Roxy, eight months pregnant, attempts suicide, and her in-laws hold her responsible for Charles-Henri's death even after his lover's husband is arrested for the murder and Isabel, the latter's suspected accomplice, is released from police custody. What is beyond doubt for the French is the national culpability of Americans: "It was an American who had killed him. I knew they were not forgetting that. Nor had his American wife been able to prevent it, with her inadequate arts. Members of a childish nation— I knew what they thought—cradle of killers and art thieves. . . . How much better, they must have been thinking, if the Marquis de Lafayette had never gone over there" (304). The custody battle provoked by the so-called art theft of a painting, Roxy's wedding gift to her husband, seriously embitters the divorce. Significantly it is a portrait of Saint Ursula, whose legendary preference for martyrdom over marriage comes to seem a wise choice in the context of the novel.

What ultimately turns out to matter most to Isabel is not the thrill of a sexual relationship with a powerful and sophisticated man fifty years her senior, an experience that superficially transforms her into a replica of a well-dressed Frenchwoman who knows what to order in Michelin-starred restaurants, but rather the change that takes place in her own perception, "the excitement of political consciousness" (141). Although Isabel frequently exhibits the naïveté and the frivolousness that one would expect in a comedy of manners, in the end *Le Divorce* is decidedly not *Sabrina* (1954) or *Funny Face* (1957). In her ongoing exploration of the multiple possibilities of the novel of manners, Johnson frames the consideration of ethical issues within a specifically political and historical context, making her third use of first-person narration particularly successful in fulfilling its intended function: "To me my heroines are neutral interpretive consciousnesses through whom to observe external political events."[9] Significantly the source of Isabel's increased knowledge and understanding of past and present world affairs is not only her liaison with a French lover but also her friendship with a second mentor, who is female and American. Isabel envies Edgar, a statesman and public intellectual, and Octavia Pace, a renowned expatriate writer, for the same reasons: "[I felt] jealous of their two minds stuffed with political facts and the confidence of their opinions. . . . I was even jealous of their age, and of their knowledge of the past—of the past I had never thought of—Vietnam, the Balkans, World War Two. . . . Why had those things never come to my notice in California?" (139).

The most timely and realistic of the novel's political references—Edgar's obsession, increasingly shared by Isabel and Roxy, with the war in Bosnia—is also the most important metaphorically. The Bosnian War (1992–1995), contemporaneous with the fictional events of Le Divorce, reproduces the interpersonal tensions of marriage and divorce on an international scale, as evidenced by the generic Romeo and Juliet image singled out by the media as the "emblem" of the conflict: "a Serb boy and Muslim girl or vice versa, lovers, shot by one side or the other in a no-man's-land as they tried to flee" (53). In keeping with Johnson's constant interest in the figurative possibilities of place, she uses the connotations of the Balkans—a region made up of so many places as to be no place at all, an artificially unified site of irreconcilable differences, an area paralyzed by the inability to move beyond national, cultural, and ethnic identities—to figure a generic version of failed multiculturalism.

This conflict is more directly embodied in the painting of Saint Ursula, an unattributed work that the Persand family nonetheless attempts to claim as "a French picture, after all" (195). This "horrible idea" gives Isabel "a glimpse into the stupid Serbs, crazed Irishmen, all those moronic brutes in the Balkans, all those fanatic Arabs in their identical costumes, all deranged by this really limiting idea, the dismal, lazy-minded habit of nationality" (195). Isabel's immediate reaction—to reject citizenship entirely and to redefine herself as "a person without a country"—is ironic, of course, since her desire to "divorce" herself from her background might well be considered a particularly compelling sign of her Americanness (309). Isabel is in fact a perfect example of Johnson's belief that Americans abroad can never escape "the obligation that is laid on every American to be an American, with all the flaws imputed to Americans by other countries."[10] Edgar, who turns out not to be "above nationality," after all (196), is one of the many characters who points this out to her at the end of the novel. His final words to Isabel take the form of a diatribe addressed to "you Americans":

> I perceived that I was being held responsible for all the deficiencies of my tribe. . . . "You mean Americans, you don't mean me," I protested.
> "You are very American, Isabel," Edgar said. (293)

In ironic contrast to the cultural tensions and divisions that characterize the representational world of *Le Divorce,* Johnson creates a complexly intercultural universe within the postmodern textual space of the novel itself. Chapter titles are replaced by an extensive network of epigraphs, which refer at once to the content of the section they introduce and to the work from which they are cited. Although epigraphs to some extent recall the intertitles used in New Wave films, the importance they place on language serves to distinguish the visual culture of the United States, which provides the model for the novel's overall structure, from the literary culture of France, which enriches its content. Thirty of a total of thirty-five epigraphs are borrowed from French writers and feature the most noted figures of the French literary canon, including Voltaire, Blaise Pascal, Michel de Montaigne, François La Rochefoucauld, Victor Hugo, Jean-Jacques Rousseau, François Rabelais, Marcel Proust, Jules Michelet, Pierre Beaumarchais, and Molière. The predominance of moralists and philosophers creates a particularly suitable context for a novel of manners, and the prevalence of epigrams and aphorisms evident in Johnson's own prose in *Le Divorce* suggests their direct influence on the writing of this one. More important, the foreign pantheon on which Johnson draws results in a contemporary American novel being significantly repositioned within a French literary tradition. Readers who follow the itinerary of the transhistorical and cross-cultural voyage outlined in *Le Divorce* are transported into an imaginary literary space beyond traditional national boundaries.

Other than the Jamesian epigraph that marks the threshold of the fiction, Johnson does not directly quote the inventor of the international novel within the text itself, though Isabel's occasional references provide amusing examples of self-reflexive signposts. Roxy's parents, for instance, fear that her marriage has delivered her "into the hands of impoverished European fortune hunters, like a victim out of Henry James" (228); the Persand family equates Isabel and her sister with what they see as a "famous type" of American girl—"they are all heiresses out to claim French husbands" (235); and the proposed sale of Saint Ursula leads the narrator to imagine herself as "Isabel the heiress" (246), although she only acknowledges Mrs. Pace's suggestion that she read "the novels of Henry James" in the penultimate sentence of her narration (305).

Even without such clues, few readers are likely to miss Johnson's internal referencing of James's *The Portrait of a Lady* (1882). Analogies of name and of situation make Isabel Walker the contemporary counterpart of Isabel Archer. Both come to Europe from America at the request of relatives but in search of knowledge of their own; both value independence and freedom; both are characterized by their charm, intelligence, curiosity, and resourcefulness; both meet with unexpected success in their new surroundings; both are befriended by expatriate American women with a secret in their pasts; both are manipulated by dishonest schemers. Both fall in love—or believe that they have. One marries unhappily and wishes she could abandon her husband; the other has an affair she is unhappy to see end and believes she will be abandoned. It may seem unreasonable to compare the one's lover to the other's husband, but in fact Oncle Edgar has something of Gilbert Osmond's character—a certain rigidity and preoccupation with form and tradition—and Edgar too actively seeks to reshape his Isabel's mind and manners. Clearly such similarities operate only at a very general level and to very different consequences. Notably a hundred years later, Isabel Walker is the narrator of her own story and the heroine of a largely comic novel. Such intertextuality acts primarily as a source of pleasure for Johnson's readers and a reminder that literature allows them to cross borders and to participate in an intercultural conversation. James's and Johnson's readers are thus invited to share the same sense of dislocation and relocation engendered in the characters who integrate a foreign culture in the novels of the two writers.

Readers of *Le Divorce* have the additional satisfaction of discovering that Johnson's novel is simultaneously indebted to a French text, Benjamin Constant's *Adolphe* (1816), whose influence within its own national canon rivals that of James within his. The thirteen epigraphs from *Adolphe,* the only source that appears more than once, foreground its significance and provide in and of themselves a sense of the novel as a whole. Because Johnson quotes from throughout Constant's work, she metaphorically re-creates his text within her own and revises both through their superimposition. Although the connections between *Le Divorce* and *Adolphe* are less direct than in the case of *The Portrait of a Lady,* the first-person narrative of an immature young man whose life and character are changed as a result of a tragic love affair with an older woman of a different nationality is clearly pertinent to understanding both Isabel and Roxy. Once the reader perceives the shadow that *Adolphe* casts over *Le Divorce,* Roxy's suicide attempt and Charles-Henri's murder no longer seem as incongruous as would otherwise be the case, particularly since some of the thirteen epigraphs refer to Isabel, some to her sister, and others to both of the young women at the same time.

In keeping with the epigraphic and the intertextual networks of *Le Divorce,* Isabel quickly replaces her initial belief that she is telling her sister's story with a more accurate description of the novel that suggestively embraces its entire cast of characters as well as all those who figure in the many texts referenced within it: "Perhaps it isn't Roxy's story so much as the story of an intersection of all our lives" (100). Not only does the key notion of an intersection provide an admirable self-reflexive metaphor for the textual space of the novel, but it is also reproduced in the emblematic places represented within it. The most important of these is an ironic version of Disneyland Paris, which functions as a dramatic and cultural crossroads in keeping with Isabel's role as a "go-between" among the "different worlds in Paris" (97). The incongruous site of both a family reunion and a hostage crisis, Isabel ironically rediscovers her native California in the French replica of the original theme park: "It was all so decorative and sweet, an idealized America, and I had to admit it was nice to be back in America, especially America refined to its ideal essence" (263). She finds herself unexpectedly at home in an equally artificial but more familiar fantasy world than the "make-believe world of France" (263) in which she has spent the last six months. At the same time, the portrayal of America and France as similarly imaginary locations, each with its own particular balance of myth and reality, supports the comparative architecture of Johnson's new international novel even as it underscores the ironic distance separating it from James's original model.

Le Mariage

Johnson conceived of *Le Mariage* (2000), the second novel in her Franco-American trilogy, as "a continuation of [her] experience of being an American in France" rather than a sequel to *Le Divorce.*[11] That the successive titles of the two works more accurately suggest a disruption, indeed a reversal, of the normal sequence of romantic events is no doubt consistent with the novelist's distinctive irony. In keeping with the cross-cultural focus of the trilogy's larger study of manners, the titular inversion of separation and union also serves to foreground the cyclical nature of the love-hate relationship that has long characterized the alliance between France and the United States. In 1995, for example, Tom Bishop described the current state of the historical association as "more that of a love affair than that of a friendship, with its passions, jealousies, idyllic moments, suspicions, break-ups, reconciliations, heartbreaks, the perpetual accusations of 'you don't love me as much as I love you.'"[12]

Given the dramatic interest inherent in such a troubled dynamic, it is not surprising that Franco-American relations have informed a steady stream of cross-cultural studies, both fictional and nonfictional, over the years. Since

Johnson's trilogy not only contributes to this ongoing cultural and literary trend but also may well have helped to revitalize it at the beginning of the twenty-first century, it is wonderfully appropriate that *Le Mariage* opens with a comic allusion to both the general phenomenon and the specific novel to come. Upon arriving at the first of the many parties she and her American fiancé will attend in the eight weeks leading up to their wedding, French bride-to-be Anne-Sophie d'Argel ponders its purpose: "Was this a reception for one of the bow ties, a famous economist or historian, was that it?—someone who had written a book, another book, about France? *Zut,* they produced them endlessly, anglophones and their books. Even Tim threatened to write one."[13] Tim Nollinger, freelance journalist and "would-be novelist" (4), feels both pressure to participate and uncertainty about the nature of his contribution: "Shouldn't he have a long project? Write a novel? What about? Or a book about European politics? All he really knew about was being in France—its history, wines, social conditions" (128).

Although *Le Divorce* and *Le Mariage* tell autonomous stories, each of which can be fully appreciated apart from the other, the additional pleasure that a new novel brings to readers familiar with Johnson's previous work is particularly evident here. The fact that the success of *Le Divorce* significantly increased the size of her audience may have encouraged the self-reflective playfulness that not only establishes a connection between her book and those of others but also characterizes the relationship between the first two novels in her trilogy. If the occasional reappearance of characters from *Le Divorce* simply reflects the relative stability of the American community in Paris, one previously secondary character returns to take on a leading role in *Le Mariage.* In an ironic remake of a central plot of the first novel, Antoine de Persand, the brother of Roxy's estranged husband, falls in love with the American expatriate Clara Holly. His initial attempt, grounded in Charles-Henri's misfortune, to resist the temptation of adultery produces the first of several embedded summaries of the action of *Le Divorce:* "'I must tell you sometime what happened in my family this past year, and you will understand why I . . . do not permit myself wild thoughts. The death of my brother, the misery of my mother, the *orphelins,* the chaos of the heritage, the problems of an aunt and uncle—all because. . . .' He sighed." (154; see also 116). Although Clara's husband, Serge Cray, will also stage the attempted murder of his wife and her lover at the end of *Le Mariage,* Johnson's revised version of similar events has an unexpectedly happy ending.

The incorporation of people and plots from the novelist's own previous work is consistent with the overall structure of *Le Mariage,* in which the inclusion of multiple characters and actions, drawing on a variety of generic conventions, simultaneously honors and parodies nineteenth-century Victorian fiction. Literary precedent ironically serves to resign Clara and Antoine to the inevitability of an affair despite the probable outcome:

> "Adultery is the great subject of nineteenth-century literature," he observed. . . .
> "I love adultery," said Clara. "A hymn to adultery." . . .
> "Madame Bovary, Anna Karenina—it always ends badly!" she suddenly remembered. (269)

Johnson pays homage in particular to a writer with whom Gordon Milne begins his history of the American comedy of manners: "One may safely say that we owe it all to Jane Austen."[14] Johnson's own opening sentence paraphrases the famous first line of Austen's *Emma:* "It was widely agreed among the other Americans in Paris that Clara Holly had the ideal life here, and people also agreed that if her good fortune had distanced her slightly from the normal lot of Americans, even from human beings generally, it hadn't made a monster of her as often seems to happen to women in her category—beautiful, rich, well married, far from her Oregon beginnings" (1).[15] Like Emma Woodhouse, Clara too will suffer a metaphoric fall from grace and learn much about herself and the world around her before she is restored to her original good fortune. The anonymous third-person narrator of *Le Mariage* specializes in judgmental assessments of her characters and comic asides to the reader that recall the voice of Henry Fielding, one of Austen's precursors, as well as Austen's own.

Johnson specifically links adultery, Victorian fiction, and social chaos in an essay on Ivan Turgenev, one of Henry James's favorite writers: "If, as someone has said, the basic subject of the nineteenth-century novel was adultery, adultery itself was used as a metaphor for the deep disorder in society; and society was the focus of the European novel."[16] Although *Le Mariage* is intentionally designed as a "silver fork" novel, Johnson's American version of the novel of manners replaces differences of social class with national and cultural divisions.[17] The conflict between French and American Parisians, revived at the end of *Le Divorce* by the arrest of Tellman for Charles-Henri's murder, reaches new heights in *Le Mariage* when local hunters, denied access to the Crays' property, arrange for Clara to be arrested on false pretenses. In a manner consistent with national stereotypes, Americans unite to defend the individual rights of U.S. citizens against "a really irrational persecution by an entire nation" (222), while the French raise the incident to the level of a foreign invasion. In the words of "a leading French intellectual," "*L'affaire Cray* . . . was a perfect example of how the innate American desire for hegemony, expressed by private citizens as much as in actions of the state, was attempting to interfere with the centuries-old traditions of France" (196). To the extent that the separate community of Americans in Paris is explicitly conceived in spatial terms as a place apart, "a world unto itself," complete with its own churches and stores, Johnson retains a version of the conventional geography of nineteenth-century fiction, divided between upstairs and downstairs; similarly contact between expatriate Americans and native Oregonians provides a new version of the traditional conflict of city and country (10).

In a more explicit use of literary influence, Anne-Sophie's deliciously misguided readings of canonical English-language works offer not only an internal reflection of both the eclectic plotlines and the cultural misinterpretations that punctuate *Le Mariage,* but also an ironic counterpoint to her impatience with Anglophone books about France. Although she has patterned her own behavior and beliefs on the sophisticated heroines of the novels written by her mother, Estelle, herself modeled on Colette, "the American community's ideal young Frenchwoman" prides herself on her ability to "read English well" (8, 41). In reality the summaries that Anne-Sophie provides of the books she reads reveal literary interpretations that are amusingly distorted by cultural bias. The omission of their titles allows Johnson's readers the initial fun of amused bewilderment followed by the pleasure of recognition. Anne-Sophie characteristically identifies with the character she most closely resembles by virtue of gender and, especially, nationality; with blissful disregard for the internal coherence of the fictional world, she assumes that the prominence thus conferred on supporting roles and secondary plots is the result of authorial intention rather than her own highly subjective preferences. Appropriately she first reports on a book by Henry James, "a man who had spent a lot of time in France" (41). Despite Anne-Sophie's comically skewed description of "a book about a French girl" with "a crush on her mother's lover," James's final Franco-American fiction, *The Ambassadors,* is readily identifiable (41). Similarly Charlotte Brontë's *Jane Eyre* becomes "the story of a little French girl, Adèle, whose rich father, a surly Englishman, had locked his poor wife in the attic and had taken up with a puny, conniving governess" (99). Anne-Sophie is particularly disturbed when "a story that had begun promisingly enough with a poor French girl . . . disappointingly veered off to become the story of the man character, Jake, who was not at all like Tim" (173). She is deeply shocked to learn that Ernest Hemingway's *The Sun Also Rises* is "required reading for every college freshman in America" (173).

Anne-Sophie's understanding of American reality is as idiosyncratic and as comical as her grasp of its literary masterpieces. Although even her fiancé describes her as "a compendium of received French ideas," she distinguishes herself from her fellow Parisians by her unreflective, albeit deeply committed, pro-Americanism, particularly remarkable at a time when Tim's compatriots are not popular or rather, as the narrator of *Le Mariage* specifies, "even less popular than usual" (171, 13). During a three-day trip to Oregon, the instrument of Johnson's satire is transformed from a bovaristic reader into an ingenuous Voltairean eyewitness. Paradoxically it is the very accuracy of her observations and the impeccability of her logic that make the conclusions Anne-Sophie reaches so amusing. Because Americans, unlike the French, stop for pedestrians, they are "wonderful drivers" (249); because malls have bookstores, America is "a nation of readers" (279–80); because cars are named Mustang or Bronco, Americans clearly share her own passion for horses: "Things equestrian seemed to be a preoccupation of the whole culture" (253). Since Johnson's comedies of manners focus on cultural differences rather than cultural hierarchies, Anne-Sophie's caricatured view of America is counterbalanced by Delia Sadler's exaggerated Francophobia; overstating the bad achieves the same comic effect as embellishing the good. It is true that Delia's short visit to Paris quickly turns into a parodic tourist nightmare, complete with stolen passport, sinister hotel, inability to communicate, unhelpful natives, police bureaucracy, a mysteriously disappearing companion, and the discovery of a corpse. Still her primary objection to the French is not their "death food," their refusal to speak English, their treatment of Algerian street sweepers, nor even her own personal disasters; it is simply their puzzling indifference to America: "America might as well not exist. No one here knows anything about America" (241).

This is an oversight that Cray intends to correct. The creative paralysis of the renowned, reclusive Hollywood director, who has not made a film for nine years, is restored by Delia's confirmation of an America rife with millennial angst and paranoia.[18] As with *Le Divorce*, Johnson once again privileges the medium of film in seeking analogies for the form of her second international novel. In the case of *Le Mariage*, cinema's explicitly spatial qualities, its expansiveness and infinite capacity to contain, reflect the selection and arrangement of the contents of her own wide-ranging novel. Cray imagines "a film of enormous sweep" that will demonstrate cinema's distinctive artistic features: "[Film] had the advantage of movement, and of width. He thought of the frame, and the screen, as infinitely wide, as expansive as the mind, did you but find the right image to fill it up" (89). The fact that Cray is a collector of ancient manuscripts and incunabula as well as faits divers highlights the significance that Johnson attaches to the act of collection and to the role of the collector.

Indeed Cray is only the most recent and the most important of Johnson's collectors, who are already present in the background and in secondary roles in *Le Divorce*. They are united by their collective presence within the metaphorical space that functions to signify and to unify the eclectic contents of both Johnson's fictional universe and the multicultural world it mirrors. In what might be aptly described as a "flea market novel," the Paris *marché aux puces* serves as a crossroads at which the multiple characters and plots of *Le Mariage* intersect. The stand where Anne-Sophie sells "horsey-artifacts" is the locus at which she and Tim cross paths with Delia, who acts as a conduit to the world of Clara and Cray (8). The site of theft and murder and a passageway for the movement of stolen goods, the flea market also becomes a crime scene. As the geographical origin of the complex interconnections that structure the thematic excess of Johnson's novel and allow the paradoxical juxtaposition of private affairs and public scandals and the coexistence of conflicting cultural traditions and points of view, the flea market also functions in *Le Mariage* as the autogenerative source of the raw material of the novel itself. In an internal duplication of this procedure, Cray treats the flea market as a vast prop room, whose contents serve not only to decorate his movie sets but also his and Clara's home. In an ironic reversal of this process, Clara is jailed for the desecration of a national monument when the paneling and fireplaces removed by the previous owner of their château turn up for sale in the *marché aux puces*. Delia's missing companion, Gabriel, literally takes up residence in a miniature version of the flea market as a whole, a warehouse that has the evocative power of France itself: "In the dim early light, it was a magic cavern, a backstage, a magician's attic. . . . This mysterious world suggested all the places Delia had never been" (27).

The second novel in Johnson's Franco-American trilogy is also structured, like the first, around an extended intertextual allusion. If James's *Portrait of a Lady* exemplifies the international novel of manners, Jean Renoir's *The Rules of the Game* (1939) is every bit its cinematic equivalent. In keeping with the "flair" expected from "a great *auteur* and *metteur en scène*," Cray entertains the guests at Tim and Anne-Sophie's rehearsal dinner with a clip from a new print of Renoir's "great classic" (291, 299).

Although the analogies between the film and the novel will have occurred to many of Johnson's readers long before they arrive at the chapter actually titled "The Rules of the Game," they are still likely to concur with Tim's initial reaction to the film Cray introduces as "an allegory of marriage": "It didn't seem a very nuptial movie. It seemed a damned strange movie to show at a wedding party" (301, 299). This impression is reinforced by Cray's decision to project a scene from the famous hunt, in which rabbits are repeatedly and graphically slaughtered, and not, as one might expect, from the costume ball that concludes the house party portrayed in the film. Or rather Cray succeeds in having it both ways, since the spectators of Renoir's film find themselves momentarily displaced into the world of the film: "For an eerie moment, they were the company in the film, this was the hall of the little marquis, these were the guests, now dressed in dinner clothes, reviewing an entertainment of which they had been a part that afternoon. An eerie effect, one that surely Cray was aware of" (300). In Renoir's film the two scenes function as mirror images, as do, on a different plane, *The Rules of the Game* and *Le Mariage.* The massacre of the rabbits foreshadows the murder of the heroine's presumed lover, and Cray, like his rival Antoine, is clearly "remembering the rest of the Renoir film" (302). As he points a shotgun at his unfaithful wife, his guests, like those in the parallel scene of *The Rules of the Game,* "continued to watch with interest, not sure this was not the beginning of a skit or entertainment" (304).

The ironic text that appears at the beginning of Renoir's film, which insists that the "film fantasy" is intended as "entertainment—not as social criticism," rejects any claim to be "a study of manners," and maintains that infidelity is not a punishable crime, turns out to apply somewhat more exactly to *Le Mariage,* if only in relation to the third point. The famously ambiguous line pronounced in *The Rules of the Game* by the character portrayed by the director himself—"everyone has his reasons"—more aptly applies to the tolerant ending of Johnson's novel. Certainly order is reestablished, but the rules themselves also appear to have been modified. At the wedding that concludes *Le Mariage,* Clara and Antoine already form an accepted couple: "Their relationship might almost be a settled thing, one of those social facts people accept with a wink, referring to the well-known Wednesdays (or whenever) of two people, married to others, whose irregular love had been sanctified by a kind of community consensus, this being France, Europe, the Old World, and almost the new millennium" (313). The new status of the lovers will be confirmed by their reappearance in the aptly named *L'Affaire,* the third novel in the trilogy.

The source of ambiguity in *Le Mariage* turns on a characteristically American concern with the pursuit of happiness. In "Must a Novel Have a Theme?," originally delivered as a public lecture, Johnson states that in the course of revision she was startled to find Clara "obsessively thinking about happiness," which in retrospect seemed to her to be one of the principal preoccupations of

the book.[19] Readers of *Le Mariage* are likely to be as puzzled by this pro-
nouncement as the author was by its discovery. Johnson's surprise—and the
general doubt about traditional thematic unity suggested by the question
mark that punctuates the title of her remarks—is reproduced within the novel.
Although Clara, like earlier heroines of Johnson's fiction, openly speculates on
the nature of happiness, she does so only in the final pages of *Le Mariage,* and
the conclusion she reaches is far from decisive: "This visceral dissolving sensation was probably happiness" (120). Moreover her reflection, which takes
place at Tim and Anne-Sophie's wedding reception, is immediately followed
by the priest's highly predictable ode to the "great happiness" of the bride and
groom, which ironically takes place in their absence. They return in time to
hear Tim's divorced father deliver an awkward, comic, and much more accurate assessment of the future of relationships in Johnson's comedies of manners: "I hope they will be as happy as the rest of us have been. Happier,
actually. Well, I shouldn't put it that way. Even happier, I should say. Well, I
mean, of course, as happy as humans can be" (322).

L'Affaire

In the third and final installment of Johnson's Franco-American trilogy, the
author's characteristic irony initially appears to be aimed directly at her own
audience. Given the evident similarity of cognate titles that identify relationships, readers are likely to assume, as did reviewers, that *L'Affaire* (2003)
focuses once again on the adulterous liaisons that drive the dramatic action
in *Le Divorce* and *Le Mariage.* The suspicion that the title is deliberately
intended as playfully misleading is reinforced by the reappearance in the third
novel of the lovers of the second, Antoine de Persand and his now very pregnant mistress, Clara Holly. In fact the polysemantic title of Johnson's tenth
work of fiction covers so broad a range of meanings that it provides in and of
itself a linguistic summary of the novel's essential concerns. Unlike the English
word *affair,* which has explicitly sexual connotations, the French word *affaire*
can also refer to a personal problem, a public scandal or controversy, a legal
case, a military conflict, a social function, and a commercial enterprise. The
particular importance of the latter is foregrounded by the epigraph from
Alexandre Dumas *fils* that precedes the first of the novel's four parts: "Les
Affaires? C'est bien simple. C'est l'argent des autres" (Business? Why, it's very
simple. Business is other people's money). In the case of *L'Affaire,* the money
in question belongs to Amy Hawkins, a newly rich dotcom executive from
Palo Alto whose brief sojourn in France to begin "a personal program of self-
perfection" turns out to be unusually hectic as parties, lawsuits, international

inheritance battles, war preparations and protests, natural disasters, and, in the end, even romantic flings spring up around her.[20]

To the extent that *l'affaire* is an inexact cognate, what the French call a *faux ami* or a "false friend," the title aptly refers to the mutual accusations that frequently characterize Franco-American relations. The two introductory epigraphs to the novel as a whole, which juxtapose contrasting views of a soulless America, immune to both "sin" and "suffering," and a galling France, whose "destiny" is "to irritate the world," establish the larger context for which Amy's individual misadventures serve as a metaphor. Within the text itself, Amy's ongoing quarrels with her political nemesis, Emile Abboud, with whom she inevitably falls in love, depend on the same figurative vocabulary privileged in the titles of Johnson's trilogy. Emile, for example, counters Amy's protestation that France "began by swearing eternal friendship" to the United States with the observation that if France has "been unfaithful recently," the "misunderstandings" and "collisions of temperament" that underlie his country's behavior are the same as those "in a marriage" (211). *L'Affaire* was published in the fall of 2003 at a time when "the well-known lover's quarrel between America and France" had been reignited as a result of French opposition to the American invasion of Iraq, resulting in intensified anti-Americanism in France and a similar rise in Francophobia in the United States.[21] Since Johnson's novel must logically have been largely completed prior to the second Iraq War and its immediate aftermath, *L'Affaire* is presumably more accurately described as prescient than as timely, although the writer's own antiwar and anti-Bush sentiments and, in particular, her dismay at French-bashing were well documented prior to the publication of the novel: "From Paris it seems like America's gone crazy. I cannot imagine the origin of a collective emotion directed against France. . . . It's just the most bizarre situation I've ever experienced in my life."[22] Regardless of its inspiration, Johnson's tenth comedy of manners is more clearly a portrait of contemporary reality than any of her previous fiction and confirms the important role that the place in which she lives and the culture that surrounds her continue to play in her work.

The avalanche that coincides with Amy's arrival at Valméri, a fictional resort in the French Alps based on Courchevel, where Johnson herself skis, unleashes European hostility to American aggression: "The rumor had reached the Hôtel Croix St. Bernard . . . that the new cataclysm today had been triggered by the vibrations from low-flying American warplanes on their way to refuel in Germany, presumably to do with the ongoing overflights of the Middle East, bombings of some unlucky Balkan country, or another of the numberless adventures the surly superpower was conducting" (7). When the two comatose victims of the avalanche—Adrian and Kerry Venn, an elderly English publisher living in France and his young American wife—turn out to be hotel guests, geological shifts combine with human volatility to precipitate a series of cataclysmic events. Amy finds herself at the center of the legal, medical, and cultural controversies that surround Adrian's death and the disposition of his property among the prospective heirs of different nationalities and conflicting interests who quickly descend on the hotel: Victoire, the illegitimate French daughter Venn has never met; Posy and Ruppert, the estranged English progeny of a previous marriage; and Harry, his infant American son. At the same time, Amy's solitary status as representative American designates her as both the target of the growing local anger against the United States and the designated defender of her native country. The consequences of the personal, political, and cultural storm that swirl through Valméri eventually take the characters back to Paris, where everyone's life is altered and Amy's original plans undergo serious revision.

In a 2003 interview, Johnson distinguishes *L'Affaire* from her previous work in a way that initially appears surprising, given the attention she always devotes to social comedy: "This one is very much more a novel of manners, very clearly a novel of manners. Less happens, it's more interior."[23] In keeping with James's equation of manners with cultures, Johnson's heroine comes to France in order to acquire "knowledge, or rather, culture, in its broadest sense," and to the extent that Amy's project is both inner-directed and ends in failure, the novelist's description proves to be entirely accurate (31). In Johnson's parody of the conventions of the bildungsroman, she creates a protagonist who is remarkably resistant to the development and change that traditionally define the genre and its heroes. In this context the flatness of Amy's character and her inability to achieve "personal roundedness" can be interpreted as an ironic allusion to E. M. Forster's classic distinction between "flat" and "round" characters (33).[24] The chasm between what Amy's words imply and the reality of what she really seeks, let alone what she actually finds, identifies her as the target of satire from the beginning of the novel. In contrast to the usual associations of culture with intellectual and aesthetic achievements, Amy takes cooking lessons and attends lectures on the history of the tablecloth. Far from being troubled by what she herself recognizes as "the shallowness of these pursuits," she openly embraces the "frivolity" of an adventure solely motivated by a comment overheard in a Seattle antique shop (31). When two older women credit Martha Stewart with the single-handed salvation of culture, threatened by a generation of "dotcommers" who do not know how to iron, set a table, or refinish furniture properly, Amy embraces housework as the endangered species of civilization itself, an idea as comically old-fashioned as the long braid in which she insists on wearing her hair (31).

Although Amy's French mentor, Géraldine Chastine, views her protégée's "somewhat unfilled mind" as "a remarkable tabula rasa ripe for European impressions" and Amy herself welcomes this mental "blankness" as "an emptiness to fill with a headier, more concentrated program of new ingredients," she ironically embarks on a stereotypically American program of self-improvement based on the acquisition of skills rather than the pursuit of knowledge or the cultivation of taste (37, 110). By definition culture is embedded in the beliefs, practices, and institutions of a particular society, and however much Amy may initially look like an empty vessel to both French eyes and her own, Johnson's heroine is in fact a virtual compendium of conventional Americanness, particularly as caricatured from abroad. At once innocent, practical, well-intentioned, adventurous, athletic, spontaneous, generous, friendly, and, of course, rich, even Amy's physical appearance seems "peculiarly American," as if her "optimist's temperament" were visibly reflected in her facial features (4). Her understandable enthusiasm for American capitalism leads to the certainty with which she proclaims America "the best country, hands down," and she consistently, if unconsciously, behaves as if money can buy anything (33). Clearly Amy is unlikely to satisfy what she considers "her patriotic duty to refute by her own example the things people were always saying about Americans, that they were too self-absorbed and had no head for history, nor any culture to speak of," given her frequent demonstration of the very faults she cites (32). Indeed she names Charles Dickens's *Tale of Two Cities* (1859) as a "French book" she has read, and her ignorance of French history is unparalleled (230). Amy is unable to respond to the astonishing charge that the Algerian War was "really the Americans' fault" for the simple reason that "she didn't know anything about the Algerian War; had never heard of one" (261–62).

The single way in which Amy's beliefs seem to diverge from traditional American values turns out to be the exception that proves the rule. She is a devotee of Prince Kropotkin's philosophy of Mutual Aid, grounded in the anti-Darwinist—and more important, anticapitalist—idea that cooperation, not competition, is the key to human progress. Her own stage of "narcissistic self-improvement," defended as "a gesture of cooperation to the world," is conceived as the necessary prelude to her plans to fund a foundation that will spread Kropotkin's ideas throughout the world (9, 266). Thus when Amy realizes that her money can pay for the medevac plane needed to transport a brain-dead Venn to a London hospital, she leaps at the chance to perform "a karmic gesture in the service of mutual aid," a mistake she comes to understand only when it is far too late to correct it (126). Good intentions could hardly go more wrong, to use a cliché worthy of the characteristic banality of Amy's own language. Her interpretive abilities are so weak and her lack of judgment so dramatic that Johnson's heroine is less an imitation than a comic travesty of the naive foreign observer of Voltaire's and Montesquieu's satirical contes. In arranging the "kidnapping of a corpse," she acts in willful ignorance of medical ethics, inheritance laws, and the contradictory wishes of Venn's children and potential heirs (131). To no one's surprise but her own, Amy's gesture of goodwill inevitably leads to conflict rather than cooperation and to resentment rather than gratitude.

Johnson clearly presents Amy's misguided use of planes and power as analogous to the actions of her native country. At lunch with the potential Venn heirs, Emile explicitly describes her interference as "another example of unilateral American meddling, with no regard for the consequences to others" (164). Following this accusation, which finally alerts Amy to the possibility that she may have been at fault, she is left to pick up the check for everyone. The significance of what initially seems an unrelated incident becomes unmistakable at that evening's memorial service for the victims of the avalanche, who now include Venn. Amy believes herself surrounded by a hostile crowd of people repeating the words "pay, pay, pay" when she mistakes *paix* for *pay*, a French desire for peace for an American need to appease. Similarly a Valméri cashier holds Amy personally responsible for America's failure to compensate the victims of the avalanche: "She had nothing to do with the avalanche, yet she was being made to take moral responsibility for it, for a whole category, a whole nation of people who also didn't have anything to do with it. It was stereotyping, it was profiling. . . . Not that she wasn't an American, but she was she, herself, not just a representative specimen of her countrymen" (138–39). Ironically not only is the belief in individualism on which Amy bases her outrage at being stereotyped no doubt the single most stereotypical of American values, but also in the course of the novel every single American character, Amy included, becomes convinced that he or she is personally responsible for setting off the avalanche that killed Adrian Venn.

In Johnson's comic allegory of nation and national identity, Emile functions as the French counterpart to Amy. In keeping with American views of the French, specifically Parisians, Victoire's husband is handsome, charming, seductive, philandering, intellectual, condescending, willfully complicated, witty, and cynical—his goal is to become "a perfect cynic," and his sense of irony is so advanced that he is unable to speak without seeming "to put words into quotation marks" (116, 44). Emile is also French anti-Americanism incarnate and the epitome of bad manners, giving a new and more literal sense

to the usual meaning of the "novel of manners." His persistent rudeness to
Amy is a professional necessity: "He has devoted considerable thought, ink,
and airwaves to the subject of cultural difference, and, as a certified French
intellectual, he had one especially dogmatic, unwavering, and largely unexamined belief, clung to with almost religious fervor: the unregenerate wickedness
of America. This naturally extended to Americans themselves" (118). Although Johnson's parody recalls any number of outspoken French media
personalities, from Bernard-Henri Lévy to Régis Debray, she may have a particular one in mind given the context of the novel. France's foreign minister in
2003, Dominique de Villepin, whose speech to the United Nations Security
Council established him as the leading European opponent of the Iraq War
and the Frenchman Americans most loved to hate, exhibited the same good
looks, broad culture, self-confidence, articulateness, and hostility to U.S. foreign policy as does Emile, who has himself risen to a position in the French
government by the end of L'Affaire.

Interestingly in Amy and Emile, Johnson has created fictional characters
who illustrate the intriguing findings of anthropologist Raymonde Carroll's
Cultural Misunderstandings: The French-American Experience, including its
provocative conclusion.[25] In keeping with Carroll's comparative study of cultural misunderstandings between the French and Americans in interpersonal
relations, Amy's sense of responsibility for Venn's death, shared by her fellow
American skiers, is explicitly raised to the level of a national character trait in
direct contrast to what Emile presents as a French tendency to avoid blame at
all costs:

> "The mysteries of culture. A French person would say, 'It's not my
> fault.'"
> "I've noticed that," said Amy. "They often say *ce n'est pas ma faute,*
> where we would think it polite to say, 'It's my fault,' even when we don't
> think it is." (276)

More controversially Carroll ends by proposing an equation between the
meaning of money or wealth in American culture and that of seduction or
sexual conquest in French culture. In both cases what is considered vulgar
in one society is in the other a common point of reference, an acceptable
topic for bragging, and a source, available to all, of upward mobility.[26]
Amy's real goal in coming to France is to "learn to be rich" (30), and Posy
finds Emile to be an irresistible lover even after she discovers he is her half
brother; his combination of "affection, admiration, and slight detachment,
as in a French film," make him a "quantum-leap improvement" over her own
countrymen (82).

The contrasting characters of Amy and Emile serve one of Johnson's primary goals in writing *L'Affaire:* "I wanted to get at that indefinable prejudice that Europeans have against America and Americans' rather strange longing for Europe and what they term 'culture,' which is certainly something that James went into endlessly."[27] Although Johnson's "hotel novel" inevitably pays tribute to such works as Vicki Baum's *Grand Hotel* (1929), Anita Brookner's *Hotel du Lac* (1995), and Thomas Mann's *The Magic Mountain* (1924), which is cited within the text, its most important intertextual reference is James's *The American* (1877). When Johnson reread James's version of the American in Paris shortly after completing her own novel, she found herself "slightly chagrined" to discover the many similarities in thematic focus between the two works.[28] Like Amy, Christopher Newman is introduced as a perfect specimen of his nationality; having made a fortune in business, he too heads for Europe to acquire culture, only to discover that the French, including the woman he loves, view him with disdain and mistrust and that money does not open every door. Appropriately, as in the other cross-cultural novels in the trilogy, Johnson also references a French text within *L'Affaire,* Stendhal's 1830 *Le Rouge et le noir: Chronique du XIXe siècle* (*The Red and the Black: A Chronicle of the 19th Century*), which Amy is perpetually in the process of reading—in English translation—without actually appearing to make much progress. Stendhal, like Johnson, combines the psychological portrait of a rather shallow protagonist with a satire of French society at a particular moment in time. *The Red and the Black,* similarly set in both the provinces and the capital, also features a flawed hero who fails to understand much about the world he sets out to conquer.

The most entertaining allusion in *L'Affaire,* however, is also the most unexpected, even to its author, who describes herself as "thrilled" to have thought of a symbol she views as "absolutely wonderful and truthful."[29] Midway through the novel, seemingly irreconcilable differences of national identity are complicated in further and unforeseen ways when the most French of icons imaginable, initially confused with "Marianne . . . Symbol of France," returns to Valméri (205). Kerry finally awakens from her coma to report having seen the figure of a woman dressed in silvery armor and carrying a shield materialize above her just before the avalanche was set off. Instantly recognized as Jeanne d'Arc by the hospital personnel, Kerry's vision undergoes rapid embellishment as local reporters, national journalists, and soon the international news media descend on the ski resort in a parody of the cult of celebrity. Emile quickly becomes a regular on CNN when he imagines an ingenious solution to explain the odd displacement to the Alps of the legendary Maid of Orléans: "The fact that she now turns up here—I suppose it is globalization" (206). As a "powerful symbol," moreover, Saint Joan is "mutable and can signify for the times, any times" (232). In 2003 her eternal ability to express "fear of the alien invader" is clearly most urgently required in the French Alps to protect France from hypothetical American warplanes and a foreign skier: "That the victim was English is perfectly consistent with tradition. . . . What could be more suitable for Jeanne to do to the English, and their avatars, the Americans, then to remove them?" (206).

Even Emile, however, cannot quite explain how an American happened to gain access to "the collective unconscious of the French," which presumably inspired Kerry's sighting, nor why one should become, as does Kerry, the idol of her own personal fan club, the Maid of Orléans Society, and even "a crazy votary of Joan of Arc" in her own right (308). Still Kerry's incarnation of a latter-day saint cannot begin to compare with the reversal of national identity involved in Amy's and the reader's gradual realization that the woman Kerry saw is none other than Amy herself. In keeping with Johnson's career-long interest in the mystery novel, focused in *L'Affaire* on the question of who killed Adrian Venn, the first details the novelist reveals, the color of Amy's silver-gray ski clothes and her whereabouts at the time of the avalanche, are essential clues to the identity of the person responsible. Only when her usual state of self-absorption is interrupted by a ray of light striking her reflection in a mirror does Amy herself become aware of "an image of glittering silver, now seeming, to her mind looking back, almost like a suit of armor, as if she herself could have been mistaken for Joan of Arc" (209). When the candles at the memorial service expose Amy's "silvery guilt" to all, she surreptitiously disposes of her silver Boegner *combinaison* and, "feeling like a criminal," flees to Paris.

Paradoxically, even as Johnson creates the most resolutely American of heroines, she playfully superimposes Amy's story on the curiously parallel history of Joan of Arc. If Amy is not literally virginal, unlike "la Pucelle d'Orléans," none of her brief relationships has ever "touched" her, and she is certainly maidenlike in her innocence and inexperience (30). Whereas Joan was directed by visions of Christian martyrs to form an army to drive the English out of France, Amy is inspired by the visionary message of a Russian prince to send an Englishman home against his relatives' wishes, one of whom complains that Amy "sees herself as a sort of savior, Joan of Arc or something" (315). Although the two women enjoy considerable success in the provinces, both of their ventures flounder in Paris. Each is betrayed by allies: Joan is abandoned by her army, and Amy is sued for thirty million dollars by Kerry, her fellow American and the only person who might have benefited from her husband's return to England. Although being burned alive as a

heretic is certainly a far more dire outcome than being resented and humili-
ated by anti-American French citizens, both Amy and Joan suffer in ways
appropriate to the particular narratives in which they appear. Thus if Amy is
not able to arouse the admiration that turns Joan into a national emblem, she
nonetheless converts Emile and comes to realize that America, if no longer the
object of her unqualified devotion, is nonetheless the only place she belongs:
"Like it or not, she was an American person from Palo Alto, there was no getting around this" (328).

The paradox that identifies Amy with the most French of French heroines
even as she simultaneously remains the most American of fictional characters
is consistent with the metaphorical location of the novel. In contrast to the
two previous works in Johnson's trilogy set in France and the United States,
L'Affaire takes places in the culturally ambiguous space epitomized by the
hotel, called the "figure of the postmodern" by James Clifford and considered
by John Tomlinson to be the principal example of the solitary, anonymous,
transient, and intermediary "nonplaces" of the globalized world.[30] Despite
Amy's initial entrancement with the national diversity of the European clientele of the Hôtel Croix St. Bernard, she comes to a similar conclusion: "The
whole time she had been here, she had been feeling like a spy, or someone in
disguise, unable to talk about her real situation in life, her conversations limited to empty social exchanges and one sexual interlude. Of course, wasn't
that the situation of any hotel guest? In a hotel, all were devoid of pasts, of
contexts, everybody interacting in the present, putting forward only as much
of themselves as necessary. Being a hotel guest was somewhat lonely, was the
truth of it" (190). Nor do things improve when Amy takes up residence in the
Paris apartment she has hired strangers to rent, furnish, and decorate in her
place. The closeness she feels to those literally forced to live on the streets
soon leads to the realization that she too "had in some way become homeless,
fitting neither here, nor, she had a suspicion, there, if ever she had" (337). In
this context Amy's parallel discovery that the knowledge she sought in France
is "nothing she couldn't learn at home" is less a rejection of cultural diversity
than it is a recognition of the growing internationalism of the contemporary
world (330).

Thus in what Amy qualifies as "almost a metaphor of her French experience," she decides to hold a farewell party, an ironic example of "mutual aid
at its sweetest," in a place of exile (333–34). She hires a fly boat with the
evocative name of *Elba* to take her guests on a dinner cruise in the Seine, the
fixed "circuit" of which equates the starting point of Amy's journey with her
final destination. In a particularly striking realization of the characteristic conclusion of the traditional novel of manners, Amy reconvenes everyone she has

met since her arrival in France, most of whom she barely knows, to re-create
the internationally diverse group of strangers who figuratively represent
Europe. Amy serves them a "moveable feast" of caviar tacos, lobster enchi-
ladas, and rare roast beef chili that in its cultural eclecticism connects North
America to Europe in a postmodern fusion of the haute cuisine of France and
the already ethnically diverse crossover cooking of California. Similarly the
final location of Johnson's heroine leaves her "on a cusp," metaphorically suspended between the Old World and the New (329). Such ambivalence is generally characteristic of the protagonists of Johnson's international novels of
manners as well as their author. "I believe Americans always do return to
America," notes one character near the end of *L'Affaire,* only to be immediately corrected by another: "On the contrary. They never seem to, once they
taste expatriation" (284).

CHAPTER 5

The Travel Novels
Persian Nights, Lulu in Marrakech

At the time of its publication, *Persian Nights,* a finalist for the National Book Award in 1988, appeared to constitute something of an anomaly in Diane Johnson's career. Her sixth novel was the first to be set outside the United States, and until the appearance of *Lulu in Marrakech* in 2008, it was also the only work to take place in an Islamic country.[1] Johnson's frequent objections to the many reviewers who introduced *Persian Nights* as her first novel in eight or nine years were based on the belief that such comments implied a long period of inactivity, which overlooked the fact that she published a biography of Dashiell Hammett, edited a collection of book reviews, and cowrote the screenplay for *The Shining* during this period. At the same time, however, and in the same interviews, Johnson also insisted on her own self-definition as primarily a writer of fiction: "I think of myself as a novelist."[2]

The appearance of *Persian Nights* was in fact delayed by historical circumstances. Johnson began the novel in Shiraz in 1978 during a three-month medical exchange that brought the writer and her husband to Iran in the days leading up to the collapse of Shah Pahlavi's regime and the return of the Ayatollah Khomeini. She subsequently put the unfinished work aside during the 1979–81 hostage crisis, marked in the United States by strong anti-Iranian sentiments, until a trip to Egypt in the early 1980s provided an opportunity to return to her interest in Islam and the Middle East. Ironically a work whose completion was originally postponed due to international politics became newly and exceptionally relevant as widespread protests in Tunisia, Egypt, and Libya in early 2011 both recalled the Iranian Revolution and raised fears that once again popular uprisings would lead not only to violent repression but also to new dictatorships. In further confirmation of what one reviewer

called the "Cassandra-like quality of good fiction," the novel, published virtually contemporaneously with the Iran-Contra Affair in the United States,
features an American engaged in illegal arms sales to Iran.[3]

Persian Nights is also distinctive within Johnson's body of work for the
particular way in which this version of her characteristic novel of manners—
"*American* manners," as she once again insisted—is also the story of Iran.[4]
The Persian context provides neither an historical backdrop nor a secondary
plotline but rather a fully developed narrative in its own right, which unfolds
in tandem with the personal adventures of Chloe Fowler and her fellow
Americans. This part of the novel functions as an intriguing political mystery
uniquely directed to the reader. Although the foreigners who reside in the
Azmani Hospital "Compound," a term that usefully serves to suggest both
voluntary isolation and intentional exclusion from what is often referred to as
"the real Iran," pay little attention to their surroundings and rarely appreciate the significance of what they do see, their passing comments provide a
series of clues to the growing popular discontent and the rapidly evolving re-
volutionary movement. In keeping with this goal, the third-person narrator of
Persian Nights regularly adopts the point of view of an unusually large number of secondary characters in addition to that of the heroine. The opening
sentences of the novel immediately introduce the important image of the veil,
which recurs throughout *Persian Nights* to figure the impenetrable enigma
that Iran represents for its American visitors and the uncomprehending
malaise they experience as a result: "'They're talking about you,' said Abbas
Mowlavi, noticing Chloe Fowler's glance behind him along the road, where
the shrouded women peered at her, the whites of their eyes gleaming balefully
out of the shadows of their veils. The veiled figures seemed to Chloe menacing, like the silhouettes of vultures, and there was menace in the unfamiliar
cadence of the murmuring voices."[5]

In actuality the women, like Abbas and indeed Chloe herself, are simply
surprised to see a woman arrive alone. When an emergency forces her physician husband to return to California, he convinces Chloe to proceed to Shiraz
on her own to take up residence in the enclosed community where visiting
doctors and a few of their privileged Iranian colleagues are sheltered from the
local population. The subsequent intermingling of the heroine's personal life
and thoughts with descriptions of her immediate surroundings and of the
tourist sites she visits produces a travelogue on the model of the autobiographical essays in *Natural Opium: Some Travelers' Tales*. In the case of
Persian Nights, however, individual and national identity are inseparable.
That Chloe at one point gives up her passport to an Iranian woman attempting to flee the country is highly ironic, since Johnson's protagonist functions

in a number of ways as an embodiment of America itself, including in this instance of deliberate "meddling" (240).

Thus in its oddity and discomfort, Chloe's situation as a single woman with no justifiable reason for being in Iran serves as an apt metaphor for the unnecessary and unwanted presence of Americans in general. The shockingly ugly and squalid living conditions that she encounters in "Villa Two," which resembles "a cell, suggesting torture, walls of cement like a dungeon," reinforce the sense that there is no appropriate place for Americans in this country, except perhaps in a literal, rather than a metaphoric, prison (4). The Iranian director of the hospital assumes that Chloe has been planted by the CIA: "Clumsy of them to put a woman spy in an Islamic country, or fiendishly clever, no clumsy; you could follow their thinking: 'These Muslims think so little of women it won't occur to them to take one seriously'" (66). Chloe, a self-defined "unfashionable" housewife who describes herself as "the most unliberated woman she knew," does not take herself very seriously, either (17). Her lifelong tendency to do "just what she wanted" (17) suggests a sense of privilege and a degree of self-importance not unlike that of American politicians, whom Jayne Phillips, in her review of *Persian Nights,* explicitly—and provocatively—compares to "the (traditional) housewives of foreign policy: limited in actual experience, isolated, dimly philanthropic, protected from catastrophe by material wealth and due process of law."[6]

Even though Chloe is somewhat embarrassed by "her easy American expectation of comfort" or, more exactly, of being "housed in luxury" (5), she, like many of her real-life counterparts, initially assumes that life in Iran will be essentially indistinguishable from that of the United States: "Of course she had not really believed Iran would be a foreign land" (93). At the same time, she also expects, with equal naïveté, that it will resemble the stereotypically beautiful and exotic kingdom she has foreseen in "her dreams of Persia" (5). Wrong on both counts, she is at once dismayed and disoriented to discover a thoroughly unfamiliar country whose citizens live in dangerously unsanitary and unstable conditions in place of the "benign region of camels, and mosques, and well-run hospitals of the American kind" of her imagination (93). Nonetheless Chloe rapidly adjusts to the agreeable "colonial life" (57) she discovers in Shiraz, where the only cultural differences are those between the rather "gloomy" members of the English Wives' Club and the "naturally more optimistic or naturally more self-centered" members of its American counterpart (178).

In the evenings Chloe joins the Americans who gather nightly, "like expatriates in a movie," in the Western-style bar of the Cyrus Hotel, conveniently built by the Shah to promote tourism (67). That the royal family summers in

Shiraz in an adjacent palace subtly conveys Johnson's critique of the ill-advised political alliances of her characters and the nation they represent. The unambiguous description of the Cyrus as "safe and neutral, like an airport lounge, international territory" clearly distances the hotel from its specific geographical setting to identify it as a distinctively postmodern "nonplace," interchangeable with all others of its kind anywhere in the world (233).[7] The hotel bar, like the clubs and the hospital compound, also provides another of the insular communities essential to the novel of manners, and the Cyrus's caricatured regulars, as their very names would predict, are the predominant focus of comedy and satire in *Persian Nights*. Chloe in fact assumes that General Ben Brigante is deliberately engaged in self-parody given "the comical way he said things he must know perfectly well to be what people would expect of a wicked American general" (141). Similarly she cannot quite believe that "the simple-rube act" of the Texan consultant Loyal Cooley, complete with tall tales, racist jokes, and complaints about the "Eyeranians," is unintentional and decides he must be a drug dealer, a narcotics agent, or a CIA spy (68). Although the theft of antiquities, which he claims are of no interest to the Shah, initially seems to justify Richard Dare's association with risk taking and adventure, the archaeologist turns out to be a plunderer of relics, a gunrunner, and perhaps a murderer.

Despite the fact that most of the American doctors have a job to perform in Iran—even Chloe has a small grant from the local university to study Sassanian pottery—they are essentially tourists. In fact the Azmani Hospital actively recruits its foreign consultants from among those who at any given time are "restless, divorcing, eager for a vacation, or wishing to see the remarkable ruins at Persepolis" (10). Dick Rothblatt, a dermatologist whose narrative perspective is subordinate only to Chloe's, fits all four criteria, as does Chloe herself by the end of the novel. Dick is also having an affair with Janie Faye, a young gynecologist who is really in love with Dr. Mowlavi, with whom Chloe also has a fling, although she is primarily involved with Hugh Monroe, a specialist in pulmonary disease whose marital status is unclear. In contrast to many of Johnson's novels of manners, in which sexual intrigue provides an innocent, if frivolous, occasion for comedy and satire, in *Persian Nights* the triviality of the Americans' concerns and the pettiness of their interests contrast sharply with the real and serious dangers faced by Iranian citizens at a time of great political upheaval; the result is a much more profound form of irony and social critique. In Shiraz alone the director of the hospital is arrested by the Shah's secret police, Azmani patients are dying from a typhoid epidemic, and Abbas is murdered. If infidelity and adultery are unexpectedly, albeit indirectly, denounced in the novel, it is not because they threaten personal relationships but because they implicitly betray a country and a people in need. When Chloe belatedly decides that she and her friends should take themselves seriously as moral agents—"It mattered, in the fabric of the world, whether a person was good or bad"—it is only to conclude, with a comic show of remorse, that "she was bad" (322).

Still despite her essential superficiality, Chloe is nonetheless a somewhat more complex character than any of her fellow Americans. She is closer to the traveler, as distinguished from the tourist, in the sense of the epigraph from Paul Bowles that prefaces Johnson's *Natural Opium:* "[An] important difference between tourist and traveler is that the former accepts his own civilization without question; not so the traveler, who compares it with the others, and rejects those elements he finds not to his liking."[8] Within a few weeks, Chloe finds herself conjuring up a stereotypical America in place of her original dream of Persia: "America itself, representing itself to her imagination as a mélange of freeways and muggers—this must be the way foreigners think about it too" (151). Realizing that the existence of a concrete material reality "did not need to be confirmed in inept photos by American ladies," she gives up photography, the defining activity of tourism (164). In the course of her two-month stay in Shiraz, Chloe comes to appreciate a different rhythm of life and to pay close attention to the sensory details of the world that surrounds her, even if her growing languorousness and increasing fascination with the veil suggest that the strangeness she savors is still very much a Western sense of the mystery and eroticism of the East. In keeping with the talent Chloe unexpectedly discovers for fitting shards together, traveling brings her a new degree of understanding of both Iran and her own self, but her knowledge remains fractured and fragmented and she ultimately cannot find all of the pieces of the puzzle.

As a result Chloe's capacity to adapt and to appreciate cultural difference is always fundamentally paradoxical. Such is the case, for example, with the "Iranian" to whom she becomes closest, a frightened puppy. On the one hand, she saves him from the harsh life of the wild dogs of Shiraz, whose attack on the xenophobic Cooley at the end of the novel is surely a metaphorical—and justifiable—form of revenge. On the other hand, by taming the timid puppy, whom she ironically calls Rustum after the Persian warrior in a Matthew Arnold poem, she has also "ruined" him by depriving him of the skills necessary to survive in his own country (299). The complicated maneuvering required to ship him back to the United States in order to save his life inevitably recalls the help offered by the U.S. government to pro-American Iranians forced to flee their homeland in the final days of the Pahlavian dynasty.

Victorian poetry also connects Chloe to Nosheen Ardeshir, the wife of an Azmani pathologist, who seeks Chloe's help in interpreting Arnold's "Empedocles on Etna," the subject of Nosheen's senior thesis at an American university. Since Chloe intends to read the Persian poets Hafez and Sa'di, albeit in translation, she finds "the symmetry of the situation" appealing (27). The heavily Westernized Nosheen, who lightens her hair, rejects the veil, dresses like a midwestern schoolgirl, and would much rather live in Cleveland than in Shiraz, is in many ways Chloe's double despite a ten-year age difference. Nosheen too is subject to the disapproving stares and hostile gestures of more conventional Iranian women. After ink is thrown at her in the bazaar—a practice reserved for "an immodest woman or a foreign woman, or just someone without her head covered"—Chloe gives Nosheen her passport in a symbolic exchange of identity (181). The blue ink used by religious fanatics indelibly stains the skin, however, in a particularly well-chosen metaphor for the inevitable fact that Nosheen, unlike Rustum, overcomes her American acculturation. The last time that Chloe sees her, she is wearing a chador and eagerly awaiting the transformation of her country into an Islamic republic. Ironically she now understands Arnold's masterpiece completely: "it applies to Iran" (307). Even as Nosheen's conversion reinforces the sense of Muslim society as strongly conventional, with strictly enforced rules and entrenched traditions that would seem to lend themselves particularly well to a novel of manners, Johnson has already given Chloe the understanding that such a work cannot be written, at least not by a foreigner: "She was cured of her American presumptions. . . . This is real, she thought with a shiver, I am not at home here" (93).

Chloe's limited knowledge makes her the representative of the reader as well as the writer. To the extent that the Americans within the novel paradoxically assume not only that the rebellion will be crushed, but also that the "old imam" in Paris will be a wonderful leader, they are fully realistic characters (56). Even the mockery of the regulars at the Cyrus Hotel is a direct reflection of the novelist's own experience in Shiraz: "How idiotic we were, drinking in the bars and commenting on everything. It was really hard to see that the shah would fall. Meanwhile we went blithely on, watering our geraniums."[9] Johnson's remarks in *Natural Opium* suggest that Chloe's particular failure to comprehend Iran is simply the inevitable outcome of any journey: "What is the traveler except a stranger? It came to me that I could not and was not expected to understand, and that this was the lot of the traveler, to pass through, unaware of the history, ignorant of the future."[10] The final section of *Persian Nights* offers the reader an especially powerful illustration of this principle.

The long-awaited expedition to Persepolis, intended to be "the summit of their enjoyment of Iran," is the first of two occasions on which the characters of *Persian Nights* are united in a climactic scene generally characteristic of the comedy of manners (245). Unlike most events in the novel, each of which is contained in a single chapter, Johnson devotes six successive chapters to the Americans' last outing so that this fictional pièce de résistance has the development, the length, and the autonomy of an independent story. If ancient ruins are an unusual setting for gatherings that more traditionally take place in dining rooms or at parties, their metaphorical importance in this case is clear. Persepolis, where the twenty-five hundred–year celebration of the Iranian monarchy was staged in 1971, is closely associated with the Shah, whose regime is on the verge of collapse at the time of the visit: "As the day of the journey approached, they had word that in Tehran one hundred thousand people had demonstrated against the Shah" (245). The highlight of the trip is the famous *son et lumière,* a performance that Chloe and her friends have almost to themselves when its threatened cancellation is narrowly averted by bribing the guards. The ultimate tourist entertainment, in which the projection of spectacular lighting effects is synchronized with amplified narration to illuminate history, provides a wonderfully ironic contrast to the total blackout, silence, and confusion that follow the performance.

Johnson's characters, isolated throughout the ruins, are metaphorically as well as literally lost and blinded during the long night that follows. Their inability to identify the armed invaders or to comprehend what they are doing not only sums up the fictional Americans' willful ignorance of current events but also represents their nation's larger failure to understand the Islamic revolution or to take responsibility for the longtime support of a corrupt regime. The intruders turn out to be Americans, who are exchanging guns for Persian artifacts in a parody of colonial plundering. When Abbas sacrifices his life to save Iran's national treasures—"Shahs, imams, all were as transient as himself, but the stones of Persepolis were Persia" (273)—Dick and Hugh are dismayed by their own cowardice, a lack of heroism explicitly condemned as a national failing: "They, American men, had not run. . . . that moment of hesitation more agonizing in retrospect than at the time. In the memory it stretched out, emblematic of all betrayals and treachery" (287). Chloe's own actions are, as usual, morally ambiguous. Although she saves a wounded man's life by dragging him into the ladies' toilet where she has spent much of the night, the setting itself undermines what Chloe melodramatically interprets as her only "chance, ever, to be heroic," especially since her subsequent refusal to open the door appears to put someone else at risk (280). Similarly Johnson's insistent association of "the bleeding" of Iran and the onset of

Chloe's period is not meant to be taken literally (286). Rather the comparison serves to emphasize the extraordinary difference in register between a natural, biological event and an act of violent social aggression; more important, it also functions as a critique of Chloe's selfish inability to see beyond her own personal needs or individual situation. Not even Abbas's death can shake her fundamentally American optimism and propensity to happiness: "Why was she cursed with a nature that could not grasp the tragic and went on with egotism and vanity in spite of her conscious wishes?" (302).

The characters of *Persian Nights* are reunited a final time in Tehran as they and "every Western person in Iran" prepare to leave the country (340). Although Chloe at last claims to feel the collective anger of the Iranian people, her rash insistence on entering a crowd of protesters in central Tehran is effectively just another sightseeing expedition; her sense of being "a part of history" comes down to the possibility of being "on television, on NBC, say" (326). It is significant that she and Hugh are soon forced to turn back in a metaphoric push against the forward flow of social change. That all the mysteries—but only the mysteries—directly involving the residents of the Azmani compound are solved only in the final pages of the novel reconfirms the Americans' ongoing inability to grasp the reality of the country they are fleeing. Chloe's repeated comparison of herself and her fellow Americans to "survivors of summer camp" is fully appropriate to the comic immaturity of their final actions (328). *Persian Nights* ends with a scene of pure farce as Westerners and wealthy Iranians battle to load up on Persian caviar in parodic contrast to the tragic struggle underway outside the airport. As Johnson, with characteristically understated humor, posited in a 1987 interview: "Being an American makes you sort of dimwitted about social unrest."[11]

As is often the case in Johnson's fiction, the formal structure of *Persian Nights* both reflects and enriches the content and meaning of the novel. The title alone combines multiple references. If the allusion to the Persian classic the *Arabian Nights* is unmistakable, it is also relatively superficial. The varied tales embedded within the frame story create an intricate and ornate configuration whose curves suggest Chloe's visual impression of the ravishing sights of Shiraz: "so voluptuously lacking in perpendiculars, so lavishly floral, vined, entwined, mirrored, filigreed, carved, inlaid, cushioned, screened" (164). The many different authors, narrators, and genres of the stories included within the ninth-century collection are also echoed in the complex voices of *Persian Nights,* whose narrative strategy is signaled out for praise by other writers. Don DeLillo, for example, told Johnson that he especially admires the novel's "mosaic of viewpoints and perceptions."[12] The equally evident reference to Montesquieu's *Persian Letters* (1721) is openly parodic. Unlike the social and political satire that fills the epistles of the two Persian noblemen traveling through France, Chloe writes short, vapid, postcardlike letters to her children: "Darling kids, So far I have seen people riding on: goats, donkeys, camels, and horses" or "Here I am in this historic city. I hope you are brushing your teeth" (40, 122). Her husband's final letter to her, which announces he is divorcing her to marry a lover she did not know he had, comically recalls the domestic disorder back home of which Montesquieu's hero is belatedly informed.

Although Joyce Johnson's conviction that Johnson "has set out to write an American version of *A Passage to India*" is textually indefensible, *Persian Nights* does contain a direct reference to E. M. Forster's 1924 novel, which is also based on the author's firsthand knowledge of the place where it is set.[13] When Chloe refuses to go into Shahpur's cave, the Azmani residents' first tourist destination, the overly intimate Dr. Yazdi suggests that she is thinking of the Marabar Caves: "When Miss Quested, finding herself alone with Dr. Aziz, imagines she has been molested. Or is molested. It is never quite clear" (84). Although the circumstances are very different, the pattern of a seemingly impenetrable mystery associated with a cave is repeated in *Persian Nights,* and the complications that ensue from the discovery of an unidentified dying man inside the cavern play out throughout the rest of the novel. Like Adela Quested, Chloe is authentically, if intermittently, curious about her surroundings and genuinely desirous to discover the "real" country to which she has traveled, though both women actually spend most of their time in exclusive clubs largely frequented by citizens of their own nations. To the extent, however, that Chloe is incapable of the moral act that defines Adela, *Persian Nights* once again parodies Forster's more serious portrait of cultural misunderstandings. Adela saves Dr. Aziz, whom she has unjustly accused of sexual aggression; as befits a comic novel, Chloe, who is delighted to be seduced by Abbas, suspects that she did not save his life when she might have.

Persian Nights is the first of Johnson's novels to use epigraphs systematically as an integral part of the text. The quatrains that introduce each chapter are all taken from Edward FitzGerald's edition of the *Rubáiyát of Omar Khayyam.* In fact since FitzGerald not only translated the *Rubáiyát* to fit his own poetic style but also revised and restructured the work as a whole, it can be considered a collaboratively authored bicultural poem, which therefore serves admirably, if artificially, to link the two cultures that interest Johnson. Although many of the quatrains of the *Rubáiyát* are often cited as autonomous verse, Johnson's use of thirty-one stanzas, out of a total of just over one hundred and in an order that does not conform to that of the original poem, cleverly reproduces Chloe's piecing together of pots from the shards that she has gathered or been given. In their new arrangement, the epigraphs of *Persian*

Nights now essentially conform to the events that unfold within each chapter of a novel in which privileged Americans admirably illustrate the carpe diem philosophy of the work as a whole. The recurrent pattern of alternating between past and present tenses throughout *Persian Nights* similarly supports the fusion of old and new. Ironically the Victorian poetry of Matthew Arnold appears much better suited to the growing "spiritual renaissance" of 1970s Iran than does a Persian literary classic (307). In imitation of FitzGerald's work and in keeping with the multiple meanings of *translation,* the reformed Nosheem is busy reinterpreting Arnold's poems in Farsi, recast as an "ancient Persian manuscript" to conceal their Western origins. At the end of the novel, a demonstrator in central Tehran hands Chloe a leaflet containing "A Verse for Our New Leader Beloved Ayatollah Khomeini," which appropriately reminds her of "the words of Matthew Arnold" (328). In a final paradoxical example of the cultural mayhem of the emergent Iran, the metaphoric birth of a new leader is celebrated in words borrowed from the last stanza of "Rugby Chapel," a British poet's tribute to his deceased father.

Lulu in Marrakech

The 2008 publication of Diane Johnson's eleventh novel, her most recent to date, marked a literary achievement in keeping with the surprisingly risky events that take place within *Lulu in Marrakech.* In a work best classified as a parodic spy novel, Johnson not only challenges assumptions based on her own comedies of manners but also undermines expectations derived from a knowledge of espionage fiction. As several reviewers noted, *Lulu in Marrakech* is more closely related to *Persian Nights* than to the Franco-American trilogy whose publication directly preceded it. Yet even if both novels tell the personal story of an American woman, whose actions and beliefs reflect those of America itself, within the changing social and political context of an Islamic country, the post-9/11 world of *Lulu in Marrakech* is a very different place from the prerevolutionary Iran of *Persian Nights,* published twenty years earlier. In what might seem a striking change from Johnson's practice of setting her fiction in her own place of residence, her eleventh novel unfolds in a city and a country in which she has never lived, despite several visits. In actuality the choice of Morocco offers further confirmation of the exceptional importance that the novelist has attached to geographical location through-out her career. For the first time, Johnson chose to travel to a particular place with the express intention of writing about it.[14] Her decision to do so can be interpreted as her response to a 1986 speech directed to the global literary community, cited in one of her book reviews, in which Edward Hoagland blames American writers for their fellow citizen's indifference to the world at large: "I would guess that five times as many have been to Tuscany as to the whole continent of Africa; that more have visited Barcelona than all of South America. . . . Much of the extraordinary ignorance of most Americans about what has been happening elsewhere . . . is due to the fact that their eyes and ears—their writers—have stayed home."[15]

Like the author of *Lulu in Marrakech,* its eponymous heroine and first-person narrator also travels to Morocco in the guise of a vacationing tourist but with an underlying—indeed, in this case, an undercover—professional responsibility. In contrast to Chloe Fowler of *Persian Nights* and Olivia Pace of *Le Divorce,* who are suspected of being spies, Lulu really does work for the CIA. Thanks to a valuable pretext in the form of Ian Drumm, the English lover and wealthy Marrakech businessman she met on her first mission in Bosnia, Lulu is assigned to locate and investigate the Moroccan-based network that finances international terrorism while she ostensibly pursues an interest in female literacy. To say that Lulu does not immediately appear to be very good at her job is at once a truism and an understatement; it is also decidedly comic. From the beginning she is set up as the satirical focus of the naïveté, misunderstanding, and fear that Johnson posits to be generally characteristic of American foreign policy in relation to the Arab and Muslim world. Although Lulu sets up a library and spends much of her time reading the CIA manuals that also frequently serve as epigraphs, she herself does not appear to be either professionally or culturally literate. In the opening sentences of the novel, she reviews the "foundation document" of her trade and introduces her own example as proof of the author's argument that "Americans are especially prone to self-deception."[16] She posits that she was recruited for her "gullibility" (1) and dismisses the "intelligence" that doubly defines the organizational category to which she is assigned—Lulu is FI/HUMINT, both "foreign intelligence" and "human intelligence"—as an "oxymoron" (2).

Although this is not the only naive narrator that Johnson has created nor the first time that she has made a protagonist the principal target of her humor, *Lulu in Marrakech* is distinctive in its combination of the two techniques. The already paradoxical position of Lulu as heroine is reinforced by the fact that her basic innocence and credulity directly counter the fundamental skepticism, thoughtful analysis, and careful observation that her professional duties presumably require. Because Lulu tells her own story, the reader is also potentially subject to the same errors and limitations that characterize the narrator's viewpoint. This effect is fortified by the unusual temporal structure of the novel, which switches back and forth from the present tense in which the story is told to the past tense of the events recounted. The deliberate awkwardness of the shifts in time is consistent with Lulu's ongoing

struggle to understand what has happened—"I still don't know, even now"—
and adds to the sense that she is not in control of her own account and therefore unable to produce a fully coherent version (2).

The reader's relationship to Johnson's narrator is further complicated by
the fact that she does not really exist. In an amusing example of the foregrounding of an artifice that is normally as covert as Lulu's mission, the novelist openly announces the fictionality of her own creation. The real name of
"Lulu Sawyer" is never revealed, nor does she even look like whoever she
might be. In comic keeping with popular lore, the "flashy blond hair" she has
adopted as part of her disguise has changed not only her appearance but also
her personality: "It seems to alter the character too, just as people think it
does" (70). In keeping with the self-referentiality of Lulu herself, the brief
allusions to her past are clearly borrowed from Johnson's own earlier fiction
and function as an ironic aside to the many fans of her Franco-American trilogy. As a young woman, Lulu, like the narrator of Le Divorce, had a love
affair with a sophisticated older man in Paris, much to the chagrin of her California parents and older sister.[17] In memory of the heroine of L'Affaire, Lulu
recalls a season spent as a "chalet girl" in Courchevel, where she too might
have encountered the English poet Robin Crumley and Posy Venn, who reap-
pear as a newly married couple in Lulu in Marrakech.

In what appears to be either a baffling oversight or willful ignorance of the
fact that "Lulu" is a false name, both the heroine's alias and the overall title
of the novel proved particularly upsetting to several reviewers. Erica Wagner,
for example, complained that Lulu's travels to Marrakech fail to live up to the
"hell of a ride" her name is presumed to promise, and her colleague Michiko
Kakutani objected to what she interpreted as a "gratuitous" reference to Lulu
in Hollywood, actress Louise Brooks's collection of autobiographical writings.[18] Although Johnson's—and therefore Lulu's—choice of a suitable identity for the "adventuress" conveyed by her "Hollywood pale, very showy,
Swedish starlet-colored" hair is no doubt more closely aligned with Wagner's
sense of the name than with Kakutani's, the latter is far from irrelevant (70).
Brooks identifies with her performance as Lulu in Pandora's Box (1929), G. W.
Pabst's adaptation of two German plays (1895, 1904) by Frank Wedekind in
which Lulu, like Johnson's heroine, is an ambiguous figure, misunderstood by
the men who call her Lulu, whose real name is never revealed. That two negative and inaccurate reviews of a generally well-received novel should have
been written by journalists from the New York Times is worthy of mention
given that the two articles on Marrakech published by the newspaper in 2010
openly exhibit the very "cultural insensitivities" attributed by Wagner to the
character that Kakutani dismissed as "a kind of Marrakech Barbie."[19] If the

representation in the *Times* of the Moroccan city as an "essential stop on the glam set's grand tour" corresponds to the frivolous world of European expatriates described in *Lulu in Marrakech,* it does so in the absence of the sense of irony, integral to Johnson's novel, that Wagner and Kakutani overlook.[20]

It would have been consistent with Johnson's humor to title the novel "Our Woman in Marrakech," not simply to anticipate the phantom existence of its narrator, whose own colleagues are trained to "deny knowing anything about [her]" (29), but also to emphasize the evident relationship between *Lulu in Marrakech* and *Our Man in Havana* (1958), Graham Greene's celebrated burlesque of spy novels. The immediate revelation of the protagonist's sex itself implicitly critiques a genre that has traditionally been the almost exclusive domain of men, both as novelists and as heroes. That Johnson's actual title also evokes the juvenile travel series aimed at girls—*Eloise in Moscow, Charlotte in Italy, Betsy and the Great World*—further announces her intention to mock what she is far from the only critic to identify as "boys' fiction."[21] In this context alone, it is difficult to explain the puzzling insistence of some reviewers on reading the novel as a straightforward—and therefore unsuccessful—example of the espionage thriller rather than as the clear parody that it is. Although Johnson's ironic intentions are made eminently clear throughout *Lulu in Marrakech,* dissatisfaction with the open ending of *The Shadow Knows* taught her that tampering with the generic conventions of popular fiction tends to irritate readers, and it is reasonable to suppose that writing a playful version of the spy novel in 2008, particularly one that includes terrorist acts directed against European tourists, is a much more difficult challenge than reinventing the detective novel.

Even Lulu's understanding of espionage comes primarily from literature, although her knowledge, unlike that of Johnson, who reads several spy novels a week, is comically second-hand.[22] Sefton Taft, her CIA handler, likes to cite Alfred Hitchcock's *Notorious* (1946) as a model, and Lulu considers Colonel Barka, her local Marrakech contact, to be "a fount of lore about the history of espionage, especially as it related to Morocco," because he can quote long sequences from *Casablanca* (1942) in addition to having "memorized the works of John Buchan and the more recent Ian Fleming and John Le Carré" (96). Since an appreciation of parody depends on the reader's ability to recognize the tradition that is being lampooned, it is not surprising that Lulu is constructed in the first place as the opposite of James Bond, Fleming's archetypal secret agent who has achieved mythic status in fiction and film. In contrast to 007, who is always equipped with the most sophisticated weapons and gadgets that advanced technology can provide, Lulu has a laptop, a bottle of secret ink, a camera, a clock radio, some wax pencils, and a "clever James Bondish fountain pen" that serves primarily to reinforce the striking difference between the two spies (29). Far from being licensed to kill, Lulu does not even have a gun, and the only car she gets to drive is a Eurocar rental van. Unlike Bond, who prefers to drink his signature martinis in luxurious social settings, Lulu finds Ian's nightly parties boring and frequently retires early to her room. In opposition to the fearless and irreproachable Bond, who lets neither his superiors nor conventional morality get in the way of his successful elimination of high-profile foreign villains, Lulu follows orders, often unexplained and seemingly inexplicable, to the letter; and when she is implicated in the accidental death of a presumed Arab terrorist, who unfortunately turns out to be an undercover French agent, her guilt and remorse literally make her physically ill for a period of several days. In general where Bond never fails, Lulu rarely succeeds; she faints while investigating a suspicious fire, and her botched attempt to steal a key turns into a farcical scene far more characteristic of Georges Feydau than of Fleming.

It is particularly in the arena of sexual exploits that Lulu fails to live up to Bond's reputation. Since she realizes that the CIA's interest in recruits who have "a fair chance of going to bed with possibly useful men, and the willingness," is not irrelevant to her own employment and since the cover for her Marrakech mission essentially consists of sleeping with Ian, Lulu paradoxically resembles a Bond girl much more than she does Bond himself (4). Moreover in contrast to 007's successful seduction of every beautiful female he has ever met, Lulu's lover not only cheats on her but has long been in love with another woman. In Johnson's novel the profile of a successful CIA recruit also includes "an interest in international affairs," and in keeping with the metaphoric possibilities of the term, *Lulu in Marrakech* cleverly foregrounds the clear parallels between secret love affairs and espionage operations (14). It does so, however, not in relation to Ian and Lulu but rather to Ian and Gazi, his married Saudi mistress, whose parallel history of clandestine rendezvous, hidden communications, useful disguises, convincing alibis, close calls, and a final dangerous escape to Spain suggest that they would make far better secret agents than Lulu, as Barka clearly implies: "'The beautiful Mata Hari,' said the colonel, who saw spies everywhere and could not be talked out of his belief in Ian's involvement in something sinister" (143). Having made the elementary mistake of falling in love with her cover and letting her personal involvement seriously hamper her professional obligations, Lulu cannot even spy successfully on her own lover, although with comic dutifulness she consults her CIA manual for help in discovering what everyone else around her already knows.

Fleming's hero may have become the most famous of fictional spies precisely because there is nothing remotely realistic about his relentlessly romantic adventures in exotic locales. Indeed Johnson's satire is all the more impressive given that Bond's amazing feats and exaggerated talents already make him something of a self-parody. In *The Spy Story,* John G. Cawelti and Bruce A. Rosenberg argue that the lives of real intelligence agents are so ordinary and uninteresting that their fictional portrayal would result in an "unforgivable commission of the imitative fallacy."[23] This appears to be the sin for which Wagner condemned Johnson, albeit on somewhat different grounds. Wagner was willing to believe that what she saw as Lulu's lack of intelligence and competence is generally representative of the intelligence community and for that very reason inexcusable to fictionalize: "This is a novel, and novels have a duty to entertain their readers in a way that reports on the failures of government agencies do not."[24] Such odd restrictions are particularly ironic in the case of *Lulu in Marrakech,* in which Johnson, in keeping with the complexity and ambiguity of clandestine actions, also satirizes a more realistic strain of spy fiction, which does of course exist in the novels of Le Carré and Greene, among others. At the same time, however, the exaggeration of a monotonous existence, largely characterized by repetitious routines, fruitless attempts to gather information, and intelligence failures, significantly alters the usual patterns and rhythms of Johnson's standard novel of manners.

Lulu quickly learns that her "frankly low-level and not very specific mission" involves days on end in which nothing happens, so that in striking contrast to the tight temporal frameworks of Johnson's other novels, the reader of *Lulu in Marrakech* is unsure not only of the month or the day but also of how much time is passing (4). From her arrival in late September until the unexpected celebration of Christmas, Lulu makes no specific mention of the date. The unusual unreality of the setting of the novel similarly conveys a sense of place that is consistent with Lulu's confinement to a stereotypical European world of luxury hotels and desert homes that exists entirely apart from the Moroccan city and surrounding villages. The novelist also caricatures the coexistence of fascination and fear in the face of the foreign that Cawelti and Rosenberg attribute to realistic spy fiction.[25] Lulu's exclamatory excitement upon arrival—"I was in North Africa! Mules and goats! Here were the waving palms!"—is soon replaced by endless questions, which convey not only her fright but also her entrenched hostility to Islam (22). Because Lulu is profoundly alone, isolated, and unsure of her own judgment, the reader's knowledge of the other people she encounters is unusually limited and often formulaic, even though *Lulu in Marrakech* has a much smaller cast of characters than most of Johnson's previous novels. Notably the culminating social event, which traditionally reunites most of the persona of the classic comedy of manners, takes place at a public concert whose audience includes a number of people whom Lulu barely knows or whom she meets for the first time. That one of them is a potential suicide bomber clearly further distorts the communal nature of similar festive occasions.[26]

In one particular area, however, realism serves to connect the novel to Johnson's previous fiction rather than to set it apart; all of the writer's work, including *Lulu in Marrakech,* is marked by a strong interest in the situation of women. The unwillingness of Lulu's superiors to share information or to protect her from the consequences of their own errors stems as much from her sex and their sexism as from her inexperience: "Was I not a foreign intelligence case officer? To [them] I was a beginner and a girl" (190). Taft suggests early on that Lulu should think of herself as "a woman in a window, watching, passive, part of the landscape" (45). In fact Lulu's general situation is directly analogous to that of the many other female characters whose lives are explored in the novel. Her movements and behavior are as limited by the restrictions imposed on women in Islamic society as are Posy's by pregnancy and postpartum depression, Gazi's by the abaya and the confinement it represents, Suma by the cult of virginity that alone determines her value, Desi by her inability to read or write. When Lulu is finally assigned a role in a "truly clandestine action," her initial gestures expose "the depth to which [she] had internalized the Islamic strictures against women" (156). Interestingly Edith Wharton, whose novels provide one of the most important models for Johnson's cross-cultural comedies of manners, is also the author of "In Morocco" (1917), a travel essay focusing on the condition of women, which appropriately serves as the source for several of the chapter epigraphs in *Lulu in Marrakech.*

In *Violent Femmes: Women as Spies in Popular Culture,* one of the rare critical works to address gender in the espionage genre, Rosie White observes not only that spying lends itself to fiction but that the reasons it does—the creation of cover stories and false identities, the dependence on disguise and dissimulation—draw on conventionally "feminine" skills.[27] In a review of a Le Carré novel, Johnson made a similar connection between the creator of the fiction and his characters, "all of whom—like writers—are caught up in disguise and charade."[28] In a final twist worthy of the facts and the fictions of espionage, Johnson's parody of the spy novel plays its last joke on the reader. The perfect circularity of *Lulu in Marrakech,* which begins and ends with the heroine in midflight on her way to an assignment, encourages a reexamination of the story that she has told, particularly in light of its conclusion. Far from being "out of character," as one reviewer complained,[29] Lulu's decision to accept a new mission in London with none other than Lord Drumm, Ian's father, as her cover is the perfect realization of the movie plot proposed as the original script for her performance:

> I thought of Taft's mention of *Notorious,* with Ian as the longed-for Cary Grant and Lord Drumm playing the Claude Rains part. In a good cause. America! I had to face facts. . . . I couldn't stay in Morocco, but I couldn't go back to France or California either, and I had to be somewhere. So I had to behave and take orders, like Ingrid Bergman.
>
> It was through this frivolous film analogy that I could see the future, and what I saw was that I had plunged so deeply into the thicket, through the dark and tangled foliage, that I couldn't avoid seeing out the other side: there was London . . . oh yes, I'd spent some time in London, it was very agreeable. (295)

This combination of a cynicism worthy of James Bond and a pragmatism characteristic of George Smiley suggest that Lulu has been surprisingly good at her job all along. All things considered, the appearance of stupidity and ineptitude provide a devilishly clever cover for espionage, and in retrospect Lulu's insistence that she "must be careful not to seem competent" seems less ironically self-mocking than shrewdly precautionary (269). Her success in deceiving the reader is hardly surprising given that no one in the novel ever suspects that she might be a spy. From the moment she agrees to visit Ian in Morocco, Lulu is actively engaged in "role-playing" and "manipulating" others (16), and she becomes increasingly skilled at disguising her own thoughts behind "outright lies" (167). In an important spatial metaphor, within a few days of roaming the labyrinthine streets of the Marrakech souk, Lulu has already "mastered its geography" (68). She feels "institutional pride" in the CIA (164), an organization in which she wants to "succeed professionally— as predicted for the paradigmatic young person sought by the agency" (4). In keeping with her real attraction, which is not to service but to adventure, Lulu comes into her own in the second half of the novel when "the endgame" begins (156). In a room full of secret agents employed by three different countries, she alone locates a suicide bomber and acts to prevent the terrorist attack planned for the concert. She has no actual compunctions about her team's planned rendition, and after the target dies, she knows that her illness is not really due to "a guilty conscience" or any other "moral qualm" but simply to "chagrin at having screwed up" (265).

Lulu's realization that she will eventually be as hardened to violence, death, and danger as her own "experienced colleagues" is fully consistent with her evolution in the course of a novel that is ultimately a clandestine bildungsro-man whose narrator tells the satirical story of how she grew up to become a spy (252). In a broader context, the end of Lulu's innocence and her contin-ued travels have positive connotations for Johnson, as she indicated in an interview contemporaneous with the publication of *Lulu in Marrakech:* "This goes to my feeling that Americans should travel more—that if we were less innocent, we would make fewer mistakes. Maybe innocence is a synonym for provincial, or clueless, but it's also egotistical of us, a sort of faux naiveté that we use as an excuse for doing whatever we please. So loss of innocence can be equated with a worldliness that would be to our benefit in dealing with other people and cultures at whatever level."[30] In a final example of Johnson's humor, she sends her most recent heroine, who has not lived in the United States for years, not only to the country responsible for producing a remark-able number of the best-known writers of espionage fiction but also to the home city of both Bond and Smiley. As Lulu notes with appropriate self-referentiality: "Brits were apt to be spies; it was they, after all, who had in-vented the term 'double-cross' and its practice" (114).

CHAPTER 6

Conclusion
The Critical Works

Although Diane Johnson is best known as a writer of fiction and views herself as a novelist first and foremost, her extensive nonfictional work is not only of considerable critical interest in its own right, but her two literary biographies and her many book reviews also reveal an aesthetics, a thematics, and a textual practice that are integral to an understanding of her work as a whole. *The True History of the First Mrs. Meredith and Other Lesser Lives*, published in 1972, has a particularly significant relationship with the two novels that immediately followed. During the year she spent in England completing the research for *Lesser Lives*, Johnson was also writing *The Shadow Knows*, which shares with the biography of Mary Ellen Meredith an explicitly feminist concern with the "lesser lives" of women and draws similarly upon the conventions of the detective novel. Like *Lying Low* in 1978, *Lesser Lives* was a finalist for the National Book Award in 1973. Nominations, let alone within five years, in what are normally two separate and distinct categories provide important evidence of Johnson's unusually wide-ranging skill as a writer; the two works are further characterized, moreover, by analogous formal innovations that together challenge the boundaries that traditionally distinguish biography and fiction. Johnson's work provides a model both for subsequent feminist biography of forgotten women and for future innovations in the literary essay. The striking originality of *Lesser Lives* no doubt explains the unusual vocabulary of compliments, not normally seen in reviews of nonfictional works, that its appearance elicited; the book is considered "enchanting," "great fun to read," and "delightful."[1]

In confirmation of Johnson's versatility, *Dashiell Hammett: A Life* (1983), published ten years after *Lesser Lives*, revealed a radically different approach to literary biography. In direct contrast to the forgotten figure of Mary Ellen Meredith, Johnson's second biography privileged the "great life" of a famous man about whom a wealth of information was available, including that already made public in an earlier biography and in three memoirs by Hammett's companion of thirty years, the equally well-known writer Lillian Hellman. In addition, Johnson's work was endorsed by Hellman, who granted the author privileged access to the large collection of Hammett's letters she had preserved. As a result, the rules that Johnson set for herself, announced in the first paragraph of the "Acknowledgments" to *Dashiell Hammett,* were the exact opposite of those that governed the writing of *Lesser Lives:* "I have not ventured to imagine or invent anything."[2] The text of the biography itself is written entirely in an objective third-person voice. At the same time, however, Johnson dealt with Hammett with characteristic irony and originality. To the consternation of a number of reviewers, the focus of her biography was not the work of the celebrated creator of Sam Spade, Ned Beaumont, the Continental Op, and the Thin Man, but rather, as its title proclaims, his "life." Furthermore, she concentrated after all on Hammett's "lesser life," the twenty-six years from 1935, when "he was done with writing," until his death in 1961 (118). As *The New Yorker* reviewer noted, "It is saying quite a bit for Miss Johnson that she is able to hold the reader's interest in this sustained anticlimax to a brilliant career."[3]

How Johnson meets this challenge contributes significantly to a greater understanding of her art and her fiction, since there are a number of revealing connections between the two writers. At the time she was working on the biography, Johnson was living in Hammett's neighborhood in San Francisco, and her own interest in detective fiction had resulted in the publication of *The Shadow Knows.* In his letters, Hammett shows the same impatience with the cerebral detectives of Poe and Conan Doyle as does the narrator of *The Shadow Knows* with the "Famous Inspector" who is their caricature, and Hammett, like Johnson, expresses particular admiration for the mysteries of George Simenon (43, 229). Hammett's twenty-nine "memoirs" of a private detective and twenty-four "suggestions" for detective story writers, quoted in their entirety in her biography, show a distinct flair for irony, comic one-liners, and generic parody reminiscent of Johnson's tone and style (44–48, 88–89). Despite Hammett's lack of formal education, he was a great reader and many of his favorite novels and novelists—*Jane Eyre, Crime and Punishment, The Three Musketeers,* Gustave Flaubert, Marcel Proust—figure among Johnson's preferences as well. The attention she pays to his appreciation for the French writers and critics André Gide and André Malraux, who praised his detective novels as serious literature, reflects her own developing interest in Franco-American differences. Most remarkably, Hammett unexpectedly turns out to share her fondness for Henry James, to whom he attributed "his conceptions of literary style and his ideas of method" (36). Like Johnson, Hammett was an articulate and intelligent author of book reviews and wrote a number of screenplays based on his own work and that of others; for many years he taught a class in creative writing.

One of the most important contributions of *Dashiell Hammett: A Life* is to illustrate Johnson's central interest in American manners and customs. In the introduction to her biography, she interprets its contradictory hero as fundamentally representative of America's "national character" and announces the overall focus she will give to his life: "All these contradictions gave his life a certain fascination, and, even more, a certain familiarity. There was something peculiarly American about it that can be better presented perhaps than summarized. At each decade of his life he did the American thing" (xvii, xx). That this "Horatio Alger"—veteran, self-made man, patriot, incarnation of America's most optimistic rags-to-riches dream—should have been accused of "un-American" activities is perhaps the greatest paradox of both Hammett's and America's existence (xxi). *Dashiell Hammett* is therefore as much a social history of the United States as it is the biography of an individual. Because Hammett himself resembled "the hero of a book," Johnson need only tell the story of this complex and enigmatic man to produce a non-fictional counterpart to one of her own novels of manners (xix). Indeed, to the extent that she situates his "heroism" in "the long blank years" of his writer's block, sustained by the carefully maintained fiction that he was working during the long hours he spent daily at one of his three typewriters, he is a prototype of Kato, the protagonist of *Fair Game,* Johnson's first novel (xxi).

In a pattern characteristic of her book reviews, Johnson ends an article on Gloria Steinem's collected essays with a broad generalization drawn from the close reading of a specific work: "Any collection of occasional writings develops an autobiographical element, an inadvertent thread of self-characterization."[4] *Terrorists and Novelists,* a 1983 finalist for the Pulitzer Prize in General Nonfiction, fulfilled the same function for Johnson herself. Initially, in the preface that introduces a collection of twenty-eight essays originally published in the *New York Times Book Review* or the *New York Review of Books* between 1975 and 1982, Johnson suggests that the life they point to is less a self-portrait than an image constructed by others: "If Oscar Wilde is right that criticism is the only form of autobiography, there is a sense, then, in which this volume is biography, made by others."[5] If Johnson's observation accurately reflects the fact that she did not choose the books she critiques beyond accepting or declining editors' proposals, she nonetheless selected and ordered the reviews included in *Terrorists and Novelists,* and the collection as a whole comes closer than anything she has yet written to representing not only an autobiography but also a theory of the novel. Her practice as a reviewer thus also respects the wish she has expressed as a novelist that critics might focus on formal and narrative concerns in assessing the interest and value of a work of a fiction. Although *Terrorists and Novelists* provides readers of Johnson's work with an easily accessible sample of her criticism, it is important to note that between 1981 and 2008 she published a dozen introductions to new critical editions and over seventy additional book reviews.

If the books that Johnson agreed to review offer further evidence of her wide-ranging curiosity, they also allowed her to pursue certain preoccupations that coincide with those of her fiction. Some of her essays are devoted to her own favorite American or English authors such as James, Edith Wharton, Jane Austen, and Emily and Charlotte Brontë. Among the European works she considers, her articles reveal a clear preference for French writers, including Colette, Stendhal, Flaubert, George Sand, and Voltaire. More generally, *Terrorists and Novelists* shows a strong interest in travel literature, in differences between men and women as both writers and readers, and in the consideration of manners, mores, and morality. Johnson's most prevalent concern remains American culture, sometimes explored through the analysis of social and historical novels such as those of Don DeLillo, Joan Didion, and Saul Bellow but also through nonfictional works dealing with such real-life events as the deaths at Jonestown and the trial of Patty Hearst. As Johnson herself became increasingly well know as a novelist, certain reviews appeared to be directly connected to specific examples of her own works. Thus, five books on Mormonism point back to *Loving Hands at Home* (1990); a book on Essalem and Californian counterculture evokes *Burning* (2007); Susan Brownmiller's polemic on rape causes Johnson to rethink the ending of *The Shadow Knows* (1982); an account of Patty Hearst's later life recalls *Lying Low;* memoirs or biographies of James's sister Alice and D. H. Lawrence's wife Frieda are reminiscent of *Lesser Lives* (1982, 1994); the introduction to Raymond Chandler's novels references *Dashiell Hammett* (2002); three books on screenplays connect to Johnson's own scriptwriting career (1990); a book about Iran brings to mind *Persian Nights* (2000); the three essays on medical matters coauthored with John Murray summon up *Health and Happiness* (1988, 2008); the many books dealing in some way with France remind readers of *Le Divorce, Le Mariage,* and *L'Affaire;* and John Le Carre's spy novel looks ahead to *Lulu in Marrakech* (2003).[6]

Even a brief consideration of Johnson's book reviews presents her readers with a sketch of the aesthetics of fiction that underlies her practice as a novelist: quest for unusual compatibility of form and content; consideration of serious social and ethical concerns, albeit in a comic or ironic mode; contribution to a greater understanding of American culture and values; originality in tone and style, narrative interest and innovation; appeal to a general audience of women and men; avoidance of self-indulgence. Her essays, which are unfailingly well-written, engaging, conversational, and learned, also display many of the same stylistic traits as her fiction, including her characteristic humor. The frequent use of the interrogative mode to raise a series of questions that might be expected to occur to others as well allows Johnson to present herself in the guise of a typical reader.

In the essays included in the third section of *Terrorists and Novelists,* Johnson addresses the congruence of fiction and nonfiction in ways reminiscent of her own literary biographies. The interest she expresses in "the enduring popularity of travel literature" also looked forward to her own contribution to this genre with the publication in 1993 of *Natural Opium: Some Travelers' Tales.* If the latter collection, which intertwines personal stories of Johnson's own life with descriptions of visits to various foreign locales, respects its prefatory principle that "travel brings us as nothing else does to a sense of ourselves," the final part of *Terrorists and Novelists* already supports Wilde's autobiographical premise about criticism.[7] The novelist's review of C. D. B. Bryan's *Friendly Fire,* which characteristically interests her less for the specific story of one soldier's death than for the reflection it invites on the moral conditions that led to the Vietnam War, takes her back to the Midwest and to the mentality of the Americans among whom she spent her childhood and youth (180). Notably, Johnson's description of Midwesterners as "deeply skeptical, not credulous" reveals the origin of what may be her own most prevalent character trait as a novelist of manners.

Johnson's respect for the stoicism and idealism of a people who stand up for their beliefs makes her unusually impatient with Bryan's patronizing rejection of those he originally presents as "prototypical Americans": "La Porte City, Iowa, is maybe an artifact, maybe a place left over from the past . . . . But it is not an imaginary place. The values the Mullens learned there should not be dismissed as if they had never existed" (191). The final essay in *Terrorists and Novelists,* devoted to another travel book, reflects a similarly romanticized and nostalgic view of Middle America. Perhaps because Mark Twain's path outlines that of Johnson's own career, her review digresses into a reflection on the only major American writer from the Midwest to have written about the region: "Even Twain, revisiting his childhood haunts along the Mississippi, had protected himself with the manners of an outsider, and had learned to speak French and German and (like nearly all the others) been living in Europe" (245.) Similarly, Johnson did not undertake her own forthcoming memoir of Moline, Illinois, until she too had lived in Paris, studied French, and written five novels set outside America.

NOTES

Chapter 1 — Understanding Diane Johnson

1. All quotations in this paragraph are from an interview with the author, March 28, 2006. Unless otherwise indicated, comments in this chapter attributed to Johnson but not directly quoted are taken from this interview.

2. Bell, "Diane Johnson," 124–25.

3. Johnson, "The Summer of '53," *New York Times Book Review,* September 17, 1995, 26.

4. Johnson, "Nostalgia," *Vogue,* September 2003, 216.

5. McCaffery, "Interview with Diane Johnson," 203.

6. All quotations and comments attributed to Johnson in this paragraph are taken from an interview with the author, November 11, 2010.

7. Interview with the author, June 17, 2003.

8. McCaffery, "Interview with Diane Johnson," 205.

9. The last two quotations in this paragraph are from an interview with the author, June 17, 2003.

10. Fine and Skenazy, introduction, 8.

11. Ibid., 8–9, 15.

12. Ibid., 14; Todd, "Diane Johnson," 122.

13. Todd, "Diane Johnson," 122.

14. Fine and Skenazy, introduction, 7.

15. Johnson, *Natural Opium,* xiii.

16. McCaffery, "Interview with Diane Johnson," 203.

17. Durham, "Interview with Diane Johnson," 205–6.

18. Todd, "Diane Johnson," 131–32.

19. Durham, "Interview with Diane Johnson," 213, 192.

20. James W. Tuttleton, *The Novel of Manners in America* (New York: Norton, 1972), 3–6.

21. Johnson, *Terrorists and Novelists,* 158–59.

22. Durham, "Interview with Diane Johnson," 213.

23. Gordon Milne, *The Sense of Society: A History of the American Novel of Manners* (Cranbury, N.J.: Associated University Presses, 1977), 273.

24. Tuttleton, *Novel of Manners,* 14.

25. Milne, *Sense of Society,* 274.

26. Bruckner, "Novelist."

27. Goldstein, "American," 15.

28. Durham, "Interview with Diane Johnson," 202.

29. Ibid., 194–95.

30. Ibid., 193.
31. Ibid., 192.
32. McCaffery, "Interview with Diane Johnson," 217.
33. Ibid., 217–18.
34. Bell, "Diane Johnson," 124.

Chapter 2 — The Southern California Novels

1. Letter from editor to Diane Johnson, April 10, 1964, Diane Johnson: Papers, ca. 1943–1997, Box 32, Folder 8, Harry Ransom Humanities Research Center (HRC), University of Texas at Austin.
2. Letter from Diane Johnson to editor, May 10, 1964, Diane Johnson: Papers, Box 32, Folder 8, HRC.
3. Letter from Diane Johnson to agent, September 15, 1963, Diane Johnson: Papers, Box 32, Folder 8, HRC.
4. Cover quote from *Wichita Eagle,* November 28, 1965, Diane Johnson: Papers, Box 32, Folder 3, HRC.
5. Johnson, *Fair Game,* 3. Subsequent references appear in parentheses in the text.
6. *Virginia Kirkus Bulletin,* August 1, 1965, Diane Johnson: Papers, Box 39, Folder 2, HRC.
7. Johnson revealed her familiarity with Friedan's work in "The Writing Life: Diane Johnson," *Washington Post,* November 30, 2008: "Years later, reading Betty Friedan's *The Feminine Mystique,* I discovered that I had been to the very school and taken the very class ('Marriage and the Family') that Friedan had chosen to exemplify the condition she was denouncing."
8. Williams, "Forum Interviews," 51.
9. Diane Johnson: Papers, Box 39, Folder 3, HRC.
10. Letter from agent to Diane Johnson, December 18, 1963, Diane Johnson: Papers, Box 32, Folder 8, HRC.
11. *Library Journal,* October 1, 1965, Diane Johnson: Papers, Box 39, Folder 2, HRC.
12. Ryan, "Novels of Diane Johnson," 56–57.
13. Interview with the author, March 28, 2006.
14. Elizabeth Berridge, Diane Johnson: Papers, Box 39, Folder 5, HRC.
15. Diane Johnson: Papers, Box 39, Folder 5, HRC.
16. Johnson, *Loving Hands at Home,* 15. Subsequent references appear in parentheses in the text.
17. *Publisher's Weekly,* August 21, 1968, 56, Diane Johnson: Papers, Box 39, Folder 5, HRC.
18. Durham, "Interview with Diane Johnson," 205–6.
19. Hayden White, *Tropics of Discourse: Essays in Cultural Criticism* (Baltimore: Johns Hopkins University Press, 1978), 83.
20. Bell, "Diane Johnson," 129.
21. Oates, "Risk-Taking," 145.
22. Johnson, *Burning,* 3. Subsequent references appear in parentheses in the text.
23. Bell, "Diane Johnson," 129.
24. Jimmy Soul advised marrying an ugly woman in his 1963 hit "If You Wanna Be Happy"; *Barney Google* was a long-running comic strip created by cartoonist Billy DeBeck in 1919; the children's song "Bingo" dates from 1923.

25. Oates, "Risk-Taking," 145.
26. Bell, "Diane Johnson," 130.
27. Ibid., 129.
28. McCaffery, "Interview with Diane Johnson," 205.
29. Arthur Pollard, *Satire* (London: Methuen, 1970), 26–27.
30. McCaffery, "Interview with Diane Johnson," 205.
31. Ibid., 207.

Chapter 3 — The Northern California Novels

1. Bell, "Diane Johnson," 129.
2. Blankley, "Clear-Cutting," 193.
3. McCaffery, "Interview with Diane Johnson," 214.
4. Bell, "Diane Johnson," 126.
5. Todd, "Diane Johnson," 125.
6. See McCaffery, "Interview with Diane Johnson," 213–14.
7. Johnson, *Shadow Knows,* 6. Subsequent references appear in parentheses in the text.
8. Todd, "Diane Johnson," 125.
9. Ibid., 132.
10. Gilbert, "Abandoned Women," 728.
11. Greil Marcus and Werner Sollors, introduction to *A New Literary History of America*, ed. Greil Marcus and Werner Sollors (Cambridge, Mass.: Belknap Press of Harvard University Press, 2009), xxvii.
12. McCaffery, "Interview with Diane Johnson," 202.
13. Sissmann, "Woman's Lot," 97.
14. "Osella, huge, fat, out of control, enacts the thin little N's rage or whatever; Ev, I'm not sure, but something about goodness and doomedness." McCaffery, "Interview with Diane Johnson," 213.
15. See Sandra M. Gilbert and Susan Gubar, *The Madwoman in the Attic: The Woman Writer and the Nineteenth-Century Literary Imagination* (New Haven: Yale University Press, 1979).
16. Todd, "Diane Johnson," 125.
17. Bell, "Diane Johnson," 127–28.
18. McCaffery, "Interview with Diane Johnson," 211.
19. Ibid., 212. See Diane Johnson, "Rape," in *Terrorists and Novelists*, 193–204.
20. McCaffery, "Interview with Diane Johnson," 211.
21. Ibid., 213.
22. In the screenplay she wrote for *The Shadow Knows* (Diane Johnson: Papers, Box 22, Folders 2–7, Harry Ransom Center, University of Texas at Austin), Johnson does solve the central mystery of "whodunit" by imposing, both in terms of romance and of closure, a version of the Hollywood ending. Andrew is still in love with the protagonist, now named "Nell," but is killed by Gavin, who intends to kill his former wife as well. Ironically Johnson solves the murder by adding yet another crime to the proliferation of those in the novel.
23. Sales, "Lioness," 52.
24. Elliott, "When Beliefs."
25. Fine and Skenazy, introduction, 9, 15.
26. Mankiewicz, "Lives," 515.

27. Johnson, *Lying Low,* 8. Subsequent references appear in parentheses in the text.

28. Chapter 2, "The Land of Plenty," references a Leonard Cohen song, and chapter 4, "Night Thoughts," an Edward Young poem.

29. Towers, "Four Days," 3.

30. McCaffery, "Interview with Diane Johnson," 203.

31. Sales, "Lioness," 53.

32. McCaffery, "Interview with Diane Johnson," 218.

33. Tom LeClair and Larry McCaffery, introduction to *Anything Can Happen: Interviews with Contemporary American Novelists,* ed. Tom LeClair and Larry McCaffery (Urbana: University of Illinois Press, 1983), 4.

34. Johnson, "First Love."

35. *Lying Low* even includes a playful parody of the kind of textual breakdown that often occurs within Robbe-Grillet's novels; after a child's disappearance, multiple and conflicting crime scenarios and potential murderers are proposed (169–76).

36. Johnson, "First Love."

37. James W. Tuttleton, *The Novel of Manners in America* (New York: Norton, 1972), xiii.

38. Todd, "Diane Johnson," 127.

39. *Health and Happiness* is Johnson's seventh novel. Her sixth, *Persian Nights,* which takes place in Iran, is discussed in chapter 5.

40. Bruckner, "Novelist."

41. Interview with the author, 17 June 2003.

42. Bell, "Fiction Chronicle," 488.

43. Ibid.

44. Diane Johnson, *Health and Happiness,* 7. Subsequent references appear in parentheses in the text.

45. David L. Hirst, *Comedy of Manners* (London: Methuen, 1979), 34.

46. Tuttleton, *Novel of Manners,* 10.

47. Bruckner, "Novelist."

48. See John Tomlinson, *Globalization and Culture* (Chicago: University of Chicago Press, 1999), 111.

49. Arthur Pollard, *Satire* (London: Methuen, 1970), 26–27.

50. Richard P. Brickner, "What's Up, Doc?," *New York Times Book Review,* September 30, 1990, 18.

51. Bruckner, "Novelist."

Chapter 4—The Franco-American Trilogy

1. Bell, "Diane Johnson," 130.

2. Rowlands, "American," 9.

3. Johnson, *Into a Paris Quarter,* 1–2.

4. Rowlands, "American," 6.

5. Johnson, *Fair Game,* 35–36.

6. Johnson, *Le Divorce,* 1. Subsequent references appear in parentheses in the text.

7. Interview with the author, March 28, 2006.

8. Edmund White, *The Married Man* (New York: Knopf, 2000), 70.

9. Johnson, "Must a Novel," 785.

10. Goldstein, "American."

11. Ibid.

12. Tom Bishop, "I Love You, Moi Non Plus," *Sub-Stance* 76/77 (1985): 21.

13. Johnson, *Le Mariage,* 11. Subsequent references appear in parentheses in the text.

14. Gordon Milne, *The Sense of Society: A History of the American Novel of Manners* (Cranbury, N.J.: Associated University Presses, 1977), 11.

15. The opening sentence of *Emma* (Cambridge: Riverside Press, 1957) reads as follows: "Emma Woodhouse, handsome, clever, and rich, with a comfortable home and happy disposition, seemed to unite some of the best blessings of existence; and had lived nearly twenty-one years in the world with very little to distress or vex her."

16. Johnson, "Triumph," 38.

17. Interview with the author, June 17, 2003.

18. The character of Serge Cray is inspired by Stanley Kubrick, with whom the novelist wrote the screenplay for *The Shining.* Cray also has two Labradors, and the realization fostered by his return to the United States to scout locations in Oregon is meant as a "little rebuke to Kubrick" (Goldstein, "American"): "By God, it's really important to have a look for yourself. The eye forgets" (249).

19. Johnson, "Must a Novel," 788.

20. Johnson, *L'Affaire,* 2. Subsequent references appear in parentheses in the text.

21. Edward Knox, "Déjà Views, How Americans Look at France: Introduction," *French Politics, Culture & Society* 21 (2003): 1.

22. Durham, "Interview with Diane Johnson," 217.

23. Interview with the author, June 17, 2003.

24. Johnson often refers in her book reviews to the theory Forster outlines in *Aspects of the Novel* (New York: Harcourt, Brace, 1927).

25. Raymonde Carroll, *Cultural Misunderstandings: The French-American Experience,* trans. Carol Volk (Chicago: University of Chicago Press, 1988), 100–119.

26. Ibid., 128–33.

27. Durham, "Interview with Diane Johnson," 202.

28. Ibid., 212.

29. Ibid., 205.

30. James Clifford, *Routes: Travel and Translation in the Late Twentieth Century* (Cambridge, Mass.: Harvard University Press, 1997), 17; John Tomlinson, *Globalization and Culture* (Chicago: University of Chicago Press, 1999), 108.

Chapter 5—The Travel Novels

1. Although *Persian Nights* was published twenty years earlier, it is closely related to *Lulu in Marrakech* in setting, theme, and genre, as reviewers of the latter novel often pointed out.

2. Phillips, "Shiraz," 8.

3. Ibid.

4. John Boudreau, "Writing Her Way to Fame," *Herald,* April 30, 1987.

5. Johnson, *Persian Nights,* 3. Subsequent references appear in parentheses in the text.

6. Phillips, "Shiraz," 8.

7. For a discussion of hotels as nonplaces, John Tomlinson, *Globalization and Culture* (Chicago: University of Chicago Press, 1999), 108.

8. Johnson, *Natural Opium.*

9. Boudreau, "Writing."

10. Johnson, *Natural Opium,* 77.

11. Phillips, "Shiraz," 8.

12. Letter from Don DeLillo to Johnson, March 31, 1986, Diane Johnson: Papers, Box 18, Folder 6, HRC.

13. Joyce Johnson, "Passage."

14. Halford, "Book Bench."

15. Johnson, "Beware," 1. Johnson's ellipses.

16. Johnson, *Lulu in Marrakech,* 1. Subsequent references appear in parentheses in the text.

17. Johnson wanted readers to be able to speculate that Lulu and Isabel Walker were in fact the same person. Interview with the author, April 14, 2011.

18. Wagner, "Expatriate," 8; Kakutani, "Goody-Two-Shoes."

19. Kakutani, "Goody-Two-Shoes."

20. Charly Wilder, "36 Hours in Marrakesh," *New York Times,* December 26, 2010; "Funky Cool Medina," *New York Times Magazine*, September 26, 2010, 75–80.

21. Johnson, "Missionary," 20. In choosing a title, Johnson might also have had the Babar series in mind. If the royal elephant rarely travels after returning from France to westernize his kingdom, his idealistic view of colonization is in marked contrast to the reality of France's colonial experience in Africa. *Lulu in Marrakech* is dedicated to the memory of Johnson's good friend Marie-Claude de Brunhoff, wife of the author of the *Babar* books.

22. Interview with the author, November 11, 2010.

23. John G. Cawelti and Bruce A. Rosenberg, *The Spy Story* (Chicago: University of Chicago Press, 1987), 59.

24. Wagner, "Expatriate," 8.

25. Cawelti and Rosenberg, *Spy Story,* 44.

26. The realism of Johnson's novel was regrettably enhanced on April 28, 2011, when a terrorist bombing in a Marrakech café frequented by international tourists killed sixteen people.

27. Rosie White, *Violent Femmes: Women as Spies in Popular Culture* (New York: Routledge, 2007), 1–2.

28. Johnson, "Missionary," 18.

29. *Kirkus Reviews,* August 15, 2008, http://www.kirkusreviews.com/book-reviews/fiction/diane-johnson/lulu-in-marrakech/?spdy=2008.

30. Halford, "Book Bench."

Chapter 6—Conclusion

1. Bernard Wolfe, *New Republic,* September 11, 1971; Robert Osermann, *National Observer,* October 28, 1972, 23; Hilton Kramer, "A Victorian Scandal," *New York Times,* January 27, 1973, 37.

2. Johnson, *Dashiell Hammett,* xiii. Subsequent references appear in parentheses in the text.

3. *New Yorker,* November 14, 1983, 205–6.

4. Johnson, "From Girl Reporter."

5. Johnson, *Terrorists and Novelists,* ix. Subsequent references appear in parentheses in the text.

6. "The Lost World of the Mormons," *New York Review of Books,* March 14, 1990; "Sex, Drugs"; "Rape," *Terrorists,* 193–204; "The Fate of Patty Hurst," *Terrorists,* 241–43; "Alice and Henry James," *Terrorists,* 68–74 and "The Constant Wife,"

New York Review of Books, September 21,1995; Raymond Chandler; "Tell, Don't Show," *New York Review of Books,* November 22, 1990, 16–18; "Behind the Veil," *New York Times,* October 22, 2000; "AIDS without End," *New York Review of Books,* August 18, 1988, "The Patient Talks Back, *New York Review of Books,* October 23, 2008, and "Will to Live," *New York Review of Books,* February 14, 2008; "Missionary."

    7. Johnson, *Natural Opium,* xiii.

BIBLIOGRAPHY

Works by Diane Johnson

NOVELS

Fair Game. New York: Harcourt, Brace & World, 1965.

Loving Hands at Home. New York: Harcourt, Brace & World, 1968.

Burning. New York: Harcourt, Brace, Jovanovich, 1971; Plume, 1998.

The Shadow Knows. New York: Knopf, 1974; London: Bodley Head, 1975; New York: Plume, 1998.

Lying Low. New York: Knopf, 1978; Plume, 1998.

Persian Nights. New York: Knopf, 1987; Plume, 1998.

Health and Happiness. New York: Knopf, 1990; Plume, 1998.

Le Divorce. New York: Dutton, 1997; Plume, 1998.

Le Mariage. New York: Dutton, 2000; Plume, 2001.

L'Affaire. New York: Dutton, 2003; Plume, 2004.

Lulu in Marrakech. New York: Dutton, 2008; Plume, 2009.

NONFICTION BOOKS

The True History of the First Mrs. Meredith and Other Lesser Lives. New York: Knopf, 1972; London: Heinemann, 1973.

Terrorists and Novelists. New York: Knopf, 1982.

Dashiell Hammett: A Life. New York: Random House, 1983; Fawcett Columbine, 1987.

Natural Opium: Some Travelers' Tales. New York: Knopf, 1993.

Into a Paris Quarter: Reine Margot's Chapel and Other Haunts of St.-Germain. Washington, D.C.: National Geographic, 2005.

SELECTED UNCOLLECTED SHORT STORIES, ESSAYS,
PRODUCED SCRIPT, FOREWORDS, AND ARTICLES

"An Apple, An Orange." *Epoch* 30 (1971): 26–40.

"Doctor Talk." *The State of the Language,* ed. Leonard Michaels and Christopher Ricks, 396–99. Berkeley: University of California Press, 1980.

The Shining, motion picture, screenplay by Johnson and Stanley Kubrick, Warner Bros., 1980.

"Aspiradora." *The Writer on Her Work: New Essays in New Territory,* ed. Janet Sternburg, 140–49. New York: Norton, 1981.

"The Importance of Plot." *The Pushcart Prize, XIV: Best of the Small Presses, 1989–1990,* ed. Bill Henderson, Sandra McPherson, and Laura Jensen, 103–16. New York: Penguin, 1990.

"Writing for the Movies Is Harder Than It Looks." *New York Times Book Review*, April 14, 1985, 1, 33–35.

"I, the Jury: Why This Novelist Can't Resist a Good Book Panel." *New York Times*, April 10, 1994.

"The Midwesterner as Artist." *Review of Contemporary Fiction* 16 (1996): 69–72.

"Ghosts." *Critical Essays on Maxine Hong Kingston*, ed. Laura E. Skandera-Trombley, 79–83. New York: Hall, 1998.

"Starting In." *Sewanee Writers on Writing*, ed. Wyatt Prunty, 92–104. Baton Rouge: Louisiana State University Press, 2000.

"The Writer as Character." *The Writing Life: The Hopwood Lectures*, ed. Nicholas Delbanco, 92–102. Ann Arbor: University of Michigan Press, 2000.

"The Most Intimate Room." *Gourmet*, March 2001, 100–112, 201.

"Must a Novel Have a Theme?" *Southern Review* 37 (2001): 779–89.

"Writing *The Shining*." *Depth of Field: Stanley Kubrick, Film, and the Uses of History*, ed. Geoffrey Cock, James Diedrick, and Glenn Perusek, 55–61. Madison: University of Wisconsin Press, 2006.

"The Writing Life: Diane Johnson." *Washington Post*, November 30, 2008.

"Some Thoughts on the Craft of Austen's *Persuasion*." *A Truth Universally Acknowledged: 33 Great Writers on Why We Read Jane Austen*, ed. Susannah Carson, 240–51. New York: Random House, 2009.

"Learning French Ways." *Paris Was Ours: Thirty-Two Writers Reflect on the City of Light*, ed. Penelope Rowlands, 11–18. Chapel Hill, N.C.: Algonquin, 2011.

SELECTED INTRODUCTIONS TO CRITICAL EDITIONS

Sand, Georges. *Mauprat*. New York: Da Capo, 1977.

Shelley, Mary. *Frankenstein*. New York: Bantam, 1991.

Brontë, Emily. *Wuthering Heights*. New York: Modern Library, 1994.

Trager, Philip. *Changing Paris: A Tour along the Seine*. Santa Fe, N.M.: Arena, 2000.

Brontë, Charlotte. *Jane Eyre*. New York: Modern Library, 2000.

Sagan, Françoise. *Bonjour Tristesse*. New York: Ecco, 2001.

Wharton, Edith. *The Custom of the Country*. New York: Modern Library, 2001.

Compton-Burnett, Ivy. *Manservant and Maidservant*. New York: New York Review of Books, 2001.

Chandler, Raymond. *Novels*. New York: Knopf, 2002.

James, Henry. *What Maisie Knew*. New York: Modern Library, 2002.

Stendhal. *The Red and the Black: A Chronicle of 1830*. New York: Modern Library, 2003.

Wharton, Edith. *The Age of Innocence*. San Francisco: Arion, 2004.

Gilbar, Steven, ed. *Americans in Paris: Great Short Stories of the City of Light*. Santa Barbara, Cal.: Capra, 2004.

Downie, David. *Paris, Paris, Journey into the City of Light: The People, the Places, and the Phenomena of Paris in Thirty Essays*. Fort Bragg, Cal.: Transatlantic, 2005.

Voltaire. *Candide*. New York: Modern Library, 2005.

Michaels, Leonard. *Sylvia: A Novel*. New York: Farrar, Straus & Giroux, 2007.

SELECTED REVIEWS

"Balloons and Abductions." Rev. of *Bloodsmoor Romance*, by Joyce Carol Oates. *New York Times Book Review*, September 5, 1982, 1.

"Story within Story within Story." Rev. of *Ararat*, by D. M. Thomas. *New York Times Book Review*, March 27, 1983, 7.

"From Girl Reporter to Feminist Leader." Rev. of *Outrageous Acts and Everyday Rebellions*, by Gloria Steinem. *New York Times Book Review*, September 4, 1983, 3.

"Darling, Darling, Hold Tight to Me." Rev. of *The Amherst Affair & Love Letters of Austin Dickinson and Mabel Loomis Todd*, ed. Polly Longsworth. *New York Times Book Review*, March 4, 1984, 3.

"Warlock." Rev. of *The Witches of Eastwick*, by John Updike. *New York Review of Books*, June 14, 1984, 3.

"First Love and Lasting Sorrow." Rev. of *The Lover*, by Marguerite Duras. *New York Times Book Review*, June 23, 1985, 1, 25.

"Conspirators." Rev. of *White Noise*, by Don DeLillo. *New York Review of Books*, March 14, 1985, 6.

"Southern Comfort." Rev. of *In Country*, by Bobbie Ann Mason, and *The Accidental Tourist*, by Anne Tyler. *New York Review of Books*, November 7, 1985, 15–17.

"Beware the Underdog." Rev. of *Tefuga* by Peter Dickinson. *New York Times Book Review*, April 20, 1986, 1, 30–31.

"Playtime." Rev. of *Cities on the Hill*, by Frances Fitzgerald. *New York Review of Books*, January 29, 1987, 3–4.

"Living Legends." Rev. of *A Sport of Nature*, by Nadine Gordimer. *New York Review of Books*, July 16, 1987, 8–9.

"Mama and Papa." Rev. of *Hemingway*, by Kenneth S. Lyon. *New York Times Book Review*, July 19, 1987, 3, 25.

"Man against His Brain." Rev. of *Memories of Amnesia*, by Lawrence Shainberg. *New York Times Book Review*, October 2, 1988, 7, 9.

"The Best of Times." Rev. of *Possession*, by A. S. Byatt. *New York Review of Books*, March 28, 1991, 35–36.

"How Mexican Is It?" Rev. of *Eclipse Fever*, by Walter Abish. *New York Review of Books*, September 23, 1993, 39–40.

"Supergirls." Rev. of *Foxfire: Confessions of a Girl Gang*, by Joyce Carol Oates. *New York Review of Books*, December 2, 1993, 25–26.

"The Summer of '53." Rev. of *Manhattan, When I Was Young* by Mary Cantwell. *New York Times Book Review*, September 17, 1995, 26.

"You're in India, Mummy, Not in New York." Rev. of *A Journey with Elsa Cloud*, by Leila Hadley. *New York Times Book Review*, June 1, 1997, 14.

"Missionary." Rev. of *Single & Single*, by John Le Carré. *New York Review of Books*, May 20, 1999, 18–20.

"Behind the Veil." Rev. of *Persian Mirrors*, by Elaine Sciolino. *New York Times Book Review*, October 22, 2000, 12.

"The Best Men?" Rev. of *The Golden Age*, by Gore Vidal. *New York Review of Books*, October 19, 2000, 21–22.

"Artist and Model." Rev. of *Loving Picasso*, by Fernande Olivier. *New York Times Book Review*, August 5, 2001, 11–12.

"Going West," Rev. of *In America*, by Susan Sontag. *New York Review of Books*, April 24, 2000, 16–18.

"Brought Up by His Critics." Rev. of *Janet, My Mother, and Me: A Memoir of Growing Up with Janet Flanner and Natalia Danesi Murray*, by William Murray. *New York Times Book Review*, March 5, 2000, 10.

"The War between Men and Women (Cont'd)." Rev. of *Mismatch: The Growing Gulf between Men and Women,* by Andrew Hacker. *New York Review of Books,* October 23, 2003, 35–37.

"False Promises." Rev. of *Where I Was From,* by Joan Didion. *New York Review of Books,* December 4, 2003, 4–6.

"Stiff Upper Lip," Rev. of *The Lemon Table,* by Julian Barnes. *New York Review of Books,* October 21, 2004, 26.

"French Revolution." Rev. of *The Judgement of Paris,* by Ross King. *New York Times Book Review,* March 26, 2006, 14.

"True Confessions." Rev. of I *Feel Bad about My Neck and Other Thoughts on Being a Woman,* by Nora Ephron. *New York Review of Books,* November 16, 2006, 12.

"Sex, Drugs and Hot Tubs." Rev. of *Esalen: America and the Religion of No Religion,* by Jeffrey J. Kripal. *New York Times Book Review,* May 6, 2007, 12.

"The Triumph of Turgenev." Rev. of *Twilight of Love: Travels with Turgenev,* by Robert Dessaix. *New York Review of Books,* March 29, 2007, 37–39.

"The Malibu Decameron." Rev. of *Ten Days in the Hills,* by Jane Smiley. *New York Review of Books,* April 26, 2007, 29–30.

"For Trophy Wives, Tarnish Is an Occupational Hazard." Rev. of *The Spare Wife,* by Alex Witchel. *New York Times,* February 12, 2008, 8.

"The Way Forward." Rev. of *The Year of the Flood,* by Margaret Atwood. *New York Review of Books,* November 5, 2009, 10–13.

"Paying the Right Kind of Attention." Rev. of *The Same River Twice,* by Ted Mooney. *New York Review of Books,* October 14, 2010, 44–45.

"West Coast Delusions." Rev. of *When the Killing's Done,* by T. Coraghessan Boyle. *New York Review of Books,* February 24, 2011, 25–26.

INTERVIEWS

Sales, Grover. "A Lioness in Our Midst." *San Francisco Chronicle,* December 10, 1978.

Bell, Susan Groag. "Diane Johnson." *Women Writers of the West Coast: Speaking of Their Lives and Careers,* ed. Marilyn Yalom, 123–37. Santa Barbara, Cal.: Capra, 1983.

McCaffery, Larry. "An Interview with Diane Johnson, October 20, 1980." *Anything Can Happen: Interviews with Contemporary American Novelists,* ed. Tom LeClair and Larry McCaffery, 199–218. Urbana: University of Illinois Press, 1983.

Todd, Janet. "Diane Johnson." *Women Writers Talking,* ed. Janet Todd, 121–32. New York: Holmes & Meir, 1983.

Bruckner, D. J. R. "Novelist with Copy Doctor on Call." *New York Times,* November 22, 1990.

Williams, Don. "The Forum Interviews Diane Johnson." *Screenwrite Now!* April 15, 1992, 47–51.

Saada, Nicolas. "*The Shining,* une histoire de famille: Entretien avec Diane Johnson, scénariste." *Cahiers du cinéma,* April 1999, 34–37.

Goldstein, Bill. "An American in . . ." *New York Times Book Review,* April 16, 2000, 10.

Fuller, Randall. "An Interview with Diane Johnson." *Missouri Review* 25 (2002): 109–23.

Rowlands, Penelope. "An American in Paris." *San Francisco Chronicle Magazine,* June 15, 2003, 9.

Durham, Carolyn A. "An Interview with Diane Johnson." *Contemporary Literature* 45 (2004): 189–217.

Halford, Macy. "The Book Bench." *New Yorker,* October 15, 2008. http://www.new yorker.com/online/blogs/books/2008/selected-emails/DianeJohnson.

PAPERS

Diane Johnson: Papers, ca. 1943–1997. Harry Ransom Humanities Research Center, University of Texas at Austin.

Works about Diane Johnson

BIOGRAPHY

Baughman, Judith S. "Diane Johnson." *Dictionary of Literary Biography Yearbook,* ed. Karen L. Rood, Jean W. Ross, and Richard Ziegfeld, 220–26. Detroit: Gale Research, 1980.

Durham, Carolyn A. "Diane Johnson." *Dictionary of Literary Biography 350: Twenty-First-Century American Novelists, Second Series,* ed. James and Wanda Giles, 161–75. Detroit: Gale Cengage Learning, 2009.

ARTICLES AND SECTIONS OF BOOKS

Blankley, Elyse. "Clear-Cutting the Western Myth: Beyond Joan Didion." *San Francisco in Fiction: Essays in a Regional Literature,* ed. David Fine and Paul Skenazy, 177–97. Albuquerque: University of New Mexico Press, 1995.

Chell, Cara. "Marriage as Metaphor: The Novels of Diane Johnson." *Portraits of Marriage in Literature,* ed. Anne C. Hargrove and Maurine Magliocco, 159–69. Macomb: Western Illinois University, 1984.

Durham, Carolyn A. "Cataclysmic Relations: Franco-American Discord in Diane Johnson's *L'Affaire.*" *Contemporary French and Francophone Studies* 8 (2004): 379–89.

———. "The Franco-American Novel of Literary Globalism: The Case of Diane Johnson." *French Politics, Culture and Society* 21 (2003): 64–80.

———. "The New International Novel: Diane Johnson's *Le Divorce* and *Le Mariage*" and "Conclusion: Diane Johnson's *L'Affaire.*" *Literary Globalism: Anglo-American Fiction Set in France,* 25–30, 193–209. Lewisburg, Pa.: Bucknell University Press, 2005.

Fine, David, and Paul Skenazy. Introduction to *San Francisco in Fiction: Essays in a Regional Literature,* ed. David Fine and Paul Skenazy, 3–20. Albuquerque: University of New Mexico Press, 1995.

Greiner, Donald J. "Joan Didion, Diane Johnson, and the Novel of Female Bonding in the 1970s." *Women without Men: Female Bonding and the American Novel of the 1980s.* Columbia: University of South Carolina Press, 1993.

Henley, Joan. "Re-Forming the Detective Story: Diane Johnson's *The Shadow Knows.*" *Clues: A Journal of Detection* 9 (1988): 87–93.

Herget, Winifred. "'Plotting Plots'—Paranoide Plotkonstruktionen im amerikanischen Roman der Gegenwart: Thomas Pynchon's *The Crying of Lot 49* und Diane Johnson's *The Shadow Knows.*" *Ethik und Moral als Problem der Literatur und Literaturwissenschaft,* ed. Jutta Zimmerman and Britta Salheiser, 229–44. Berlin: Duncker & Humblot, 2006.

Melley, Timothy. "'Stalked by Love': Female Paranoia and the Stalker Novel." *Differences: A Journal of Feminist Cultural Studies* 8 (1996): 68–100.

Ryan, Marjorie. "The Novels of Diane Johnson." *Critique: Studies in Modern Fiction* 16 (1974): 53–63.

SELECTED REVIEWS

Fair Game

Diane Johnson: Papers, ca. 1943–1997. Harry Ransom Humanities Research Center. Box 39, Folder 2.

Loving Hands at Home

Diane Johnson: Papers, ca. 1943–1997. Harry Ransom Humanities Research Center. Box 39, Folder 5.

Burning

McHale, Tom. "Los Angeles à la Sodom and Gomorrah." *New York Times Book Review,* September 5, 1971, 6.
Oates, Joyce Carol. "Risk-Taking." *Partisan Review* 40 (1973): 145.

The Shadow Knows

Gilbert, Sandra M. "Abandoned Women, in All Senses." *Nation,* June 1975, 728–31.
Roosevelt, Karyl. "Here Is a Woman with a Lot of Trouble." *New York Times Book Review,* December 22, 1974, 6.
Sissmann, L. E. "Woman's Lot." *New Yorker,* March 3, 1975, 97.
Yardley, Jonathan. "What Evil Lurks . . . ," *Washington Post Book World,* December 22, 1974, 1.

Lying Low

J. B. Rev. of *Lying Low. New Republic,* November 16, 1978, 39.
Gordon, Mary. "Hostages to Terror." *Washington Post Book World,* November 26, 1978.
Elliott, Janice. "When Beliefs Are out of Date." *Sunday Telegraph,* April 15, 1979.
Mankiewicz, Jane. "Lives at Risk." *Nation,* November 11, 1978, 515.
Politt, Katha. "Midlife Writing." *Saturday Review,* October 28, 1978, 43–44.
Rosencrance, Barbara. "Imagination of Horror." *Partisan Review* 48 (1981): 639–42.
Towers, Robert. "Four Days of Four Lives." *New York Times Book Review,* November 19, 1978, 3, 70.

Persian Nights

Dinnage, Rosemary. "Unguided Tour." *New York Review of Books,* April 23, 1986, 14.
Gray, Paul. "Onlookers at a Revolution." *Time,* March 23, 1987, 83.
Iyer, Pico. "Tourists at Home." *Partisan Review* 55 (1988): 692–99.
Johnson, Joyce. "A Passage to Iran." *Washington Post Book World,* March 22, 1987, 1, 13.
Lehmann-Haupt, Christopher. Rev. of *Persian Nights. New York Times,* March 16, 1986.
Phillips, Jayne Anne. "The Shiraz Quartet." *New York Times Book Review,* April 5, 1987, 8.

Health and Happiness

Bell, Pearl K. "Fiction Chronicle." *Partisan Review* 58 (1991): 488.
Brickner, Richard P. "What's Up, Doc?" *New York Times Book Review*, September 30, 1990, 18.
Kakutani, Michiko. "An Ensemble Piece on Hospital Life." *New York Times*, September, 28, 1990.
Storace, Patricia. "Betrayals." *New York Review of Books*, January 31, 1991, 18–21.

Le Divorce

Annan, Gabriele. "An International Episode." *New York Review of Books*, February 6, 1997, 16–17.
Bradbury, Malcolm. "The Customs of the Country." *New York Times Book Review*, February 2, 1997, 10.
Duchene, Anne. "Overheard in the cinquième." *Times Literary Supplement*, January 24, 1997, 23.
Lehmann-Haupt, Christopher. "When French-American Family Ties Get Knotty." *New York Times*, January 23, 1997, 21.

Le Mariage

Goreau, Angeline. "La Différence." *New York Times*, April 16, 2000, 8–10.
Hawthorne, Mary. "Vive la Différence." *New Yorker*, April 10, 2000, 91–92.
Lehmann-Haupt, Christopher. "A French Connection, Under Stress." *New York Times*, March 30, 2000.
Schine, Cathleen. "A Tale of Two Countries." *New York Review of Books*, May 25, 2000, 29.

L'Affaire

Dirda, Michael. "'L'Affaire' by Diane Johnson." *Washington Post*, September 28, 2003.
James, Caryn. "An American in Valméri." *New York Times Book Review*, October 12, 2003, 9.
Kakutani, Michiko. "A Sojourn at a French Inn Tests a Meddler's Mettle." *New York Times*, September 19, 2003.
Rakoff, Joanna Smith. "A Sentimental Education." *Newsday*, September 21, 2003.
Schuessler, Jennifer. "Vive la Différence." *New York Review of Books*, December 18, 2003, 30.

Lulu in Marrakech

Kakutani, Michiko. "A Goody-Two-Shoes Trips the Spy Fantastic." *New York Times*, October 24, 2008.
Prose, Francine. "Waking Up to a Nightmare." *New York Review of Books*, December 4, 2008, 41–43.
Wagner, Erica. "Expatriate Game." *New York Times*, October 26, 2008.
Weeks, Brigitte. "The Reluctant Spy." *Washington Post*, November 9, 2008.

INDEX